PFAPA: Sierra's Story

A COLLECTION OF PERSONAL STORIES, INFORMATION AND RESOURCES FOR FAMILIES COPING WITH PFAPA

Written by:
Jennifer Sheasgreen

Published by Lulu.com

Printed in the United States of America.
Select photos in the book by Angela Beckley.

ISBN   978-0-557-86361-7

This book is dedicated to Sierra's Doctors; Dr. Joyce Endo and Dr. John Paisley and my family; Dean, my supportive and loving husband, and all of my wonderful children, daughters, Shelby and Sierra, and step-children, Erin and Ian. Additionally, I'd like to thank my Mother, Connie Greening, for her endless support and encouragement as our family endured these trying times.

I especially dedicate this journey to Sierra, my youngest, and the many children and their families who have suffered with the PFAPA diagnosis. Thank you to the following children whose parents opted to share their story:

Emma
Randi
Theo
Landon
Cade
Shannon
Sami

Foreword

This book about PFAPA is well written and a good resource for parents of a child with this problem. I am personally very grateful to Drs. Marshall and Edwards who were some of the first to describe this and begin to inform the medical community. Before that, I can assure you a lot of children's doctors were puzzled and frustrated by these high recurring fevers in an otherwise well child.

Now we need to get this information out to everyone who takes care of children so they can consider PFAPA as early as possible in evaluating a child with frequent fevers and this book can certainly help.

- John Paisley, MD
The Children's Hospital at Legacy Emanuel
Portland, OR

Preface

PFAPA (Periodic Fever, Apthous Stomatitis, Pharyngitis, and Adenopathy) is a frustrating and debilitating condition which has affected many children and continues to affect children and some adults across the globe. Unfortunately, this diagnosis and its treatment options are not widely known and information about PFAPA is limited to medical journal articles and studies. Some of these studies are referenced in the *Medical Research and Articles* section of this book

This book was written for PFAPA families so that PFAPA information, personal stories and other resources can be readily available to help you and your child cope with recurring fever episodes.

I am not a doctor and this book is not intended to diagnose or treat your child. I am Mother to Sierra, who was diagnosed in 2001 and suffered through PFAPA for four years. I found that medical journal articles were not easy to fully comprehend in terms of Sierra's care and were written by physicians for physicians.

As a result, I wrote this book with families in mind, to shed some light on PFAPA, to hear other stories, to be aware of the various treatment options and more importantly, to hopefully learn how to cope as a family when dealing with PFAPA. This book includes real stories from families that have or continue to suffer with a PFAPA diagnosis and the different paths taken in order to help their child. Unfortunately today, there is not one right course, but being armed with the information to discuss as a family and to present to your pediatric physician will hopefully assist you in making an informed decision for your child's treatment options.

Table of Contents

1. What is PFAPA?

PFAPA is a medical acronym for "Periodic Fever, Aphthous Stomatitis, Pharyngitis and Adenopathy" also commonly referred to as periodic fever syndrome of unknown origin. As a parent or caregiver to a child suspected of having PFAPA, this may sound like a daunting diagnosis, especially the part of the unknown origin and medical terms that are not familiar to most parents.

PFAPA was first presented as a diagnosis by Dr. Kathryn M. Edwards, professor of Pediatrics, Dr. Alexander R. Lawton, professor of Pediatrics, and Dr. Gary Marshall Jr. from the University of Louisville, in 1987. The diagnosis was initially called "Marshall's Syndrome" and later changed to PFAPA.[1] Although PFAPA was first discovered as a condition in 1987, it is suspected that children have suffered with this illness long before the diagnosis was recognized. The PFAPA diagnosis has created questions and frustrations from parents around the globe, as there is still no sure cure for PFAPA, or any true test that can determine with certainty that PFAPA is the correct diagnosis.

PFAPA can be described as one of the most common types of periodic fever syndromes in children; however, many physicians still aren't familiar with the condition. There is no textbook definition of PFAPA, as symptoms tend to vary slightly by child although there are common symptoms that most PFAPA diagnosed children tend to display. With each particular case, periodic fevers are the one common trait associated with PFAPA, though the frequency can vary depending upon the child.

❖   ❖

Breaking down the symptoms

Symptoms known to be associated with PFAPA can be broken down into non-medical terms, which are representative of the diagnosis[2]:

1) Periodic Fever: fevers occurring on a regular basis that last from two to six days and recur every three to eight weeks.
2) Aphthous stomatitis: canker sores, or small ulcers also called mouth sores, inside the mouth on the inner cheeks, inner lips or tongue.
3) Pharyngitis: inflammation of the neck and throat to include the tonsils or larynx. This inflammation may be visible to the eye, but in the case of PFAPA, usually comes up as a negative finding on a strep test. The symptom may appear as a sore throat.
4) Adenitis: inflammation of a gland or lymph node, which has the tendency to become enlarged or tender.

PFAPA diagnosed children, in addition to the above symptoms, may also complain of joint pain, headaches, lethargy, abdominal pain, chills, vomiting and febrile seizures, though febrile seizures are not common in all PFAPA diagnosed children. According to the National Institute of Neurological Disorders and Stroke, febrile seizures are convulsions brought on by a fever in infants or small children. Seizures may be as mild as twitches in a portion of the body or the child may lose consciousness and shake. These seizures may last as little as a few seconds or as long as fifteen minutes or more.

Although seizures in PFAPA diagnosed children don't seem to be common, they have been reported by PFAPA parents when their child's fever spikes to a very high level. As you will see in Sierra's story, dealing with a febrile seizure for the first time can be quite frightening.

10

Arming yourself with information on febrile seizures, how to spot one when it occurs, and what to do about it, can help you cope if the situation ever arises.

While individual PFAPA diagnosed children may present different symptoms (some children complain of horrible abdominal pain and leg cramps, fatigue, swollen eyes, throat pain, dark circles under your child's eyes, loss of appetite, and occasional rage), the common symptom in each case is the periodic fevers.

Medical Case Study

In a study performed by Dr. Greg Licameli, MD, MHCM[3], a pioneer in the PFAPA research field, along with his team, mentioned in the footnotes, 27 children with PFAPA (14 female and 13 male) had their tonsils and in some cases, both tonsils and adenoids removed. The purpose of the study was to assess whether or not the tonsillectomy or T&A was a cure for the PFAPA diagnosed children. The result of the study showed that 26 out of the 27 children were cured after the surgery and provided a recommendation that surgery be performed for children diagnosed with PFAPA who do not respond to medical management.

There are additional PFAPA studies, some of which are referenced in the *Medical Research and Articles* section of this book. Unfortunately, no study has concluded beyond doubt that a tonsillectomy or T&A is the conclusive cure for PFAPA patients. You and your child's doctor should determine the specific path of medical management.

Predictability of episodes

Many parents of PFAPA diagnosed children have learned to predict when the next fever will strike their child. Some PFAPA diagnosed children are even able to communicate the arrival of their next cycle within days prior to a fever. When Sierra started to feel run down, she would sometimes communicate that she was getting sick again. Other times, a change in her mood and a glance at the calendar was our indication that the fever was rearing its ugly head again. The predictability of Sierra's fevers was fairly common at one point during her PFAPA period. This predictability of many PFAPA episodes seems to be a common comment among many PFAPA parents.

Tracking your child's fevers on a fever log may help to predict your child's cycle. However, a PFAPA diagnosed child may go through a period of predictable recurrent fevers and then experience a few months without any fevers at all. Tracking fever cycles also helps you notice symptoms, mood changes or other factors that may have otherwise be overlooked. The charting of other behavior symptoms may enable you to better predict the episode. Some families are able to plan events and vacations around the predictability of this illness due to the recurrent nature.

Since PFAPA symptoms may present themselves a bit differently in each child, it is not uncommon for a PFAPA diagnosed child to skip a fever cycle or two or more and then gravitate back to a regular frequency. Some PFAPA diagnosed children have even been known to skip cycles during the summer months, possibly because it is a less stressful or busy period for the children.

❖　　❖

PFAPA and stress

It is thought by many parents of PFAPA diagnosed children that an episode can be triggered by stress. There does not appear to be any studies available on this particular aspect of PFAPA; however, there does seem to be some correlation to stress and the fever cycles in some PFAPA diagnosed children. Stress can present itself in many forms. Stress could be the result of anxiety related to your child's first day of school, or a change in your household situation such as a birth of a new sibling, or a child going through a divorce and having to adjust to a new custody schedule, or stress to your child's physical body, such as severely cold temperatures, while playing in a cold ocean.

With Sierra, there seemed to be a correlation to stress in a few of her episodes. In those instances, PFAPA presented itself within 6 hours. I don't feel that stress was a factor in each of her episodes, though it's an aspect that should be evaluated by parents.

Genetic Link

Currently, there aren't any studies reviewing hereditary or genetic links with PFAPA diagnosed children. There are studies available on the genetic relationships of recurrent fevers in general, but the studies encompass patients that have fever syndromes that are unrelated to PFAPA. Some PFAPA parents believe there could be a hereditary link given the history of generational tonsillectomies and childhood fever episodes in their family prior to PFAPA being an actual diagnosis.

In Sierra's case, she happens to be the third generation of direct family members that have undergone a tonsillectomy. Perhaps it is purely coincidental or maybe there's an actual link? It is likely the direct genetic relationship won't be validated for some time.

2. Diagnosing PFAPA

Diagnosing PFAPA presents various challenges. PFAPA appears to be an illness of exclusion, meaning your child's physician needs to rule out other diagnoses and confirm the periodic nature of the fever before a PFAPA diagnosis is confirmed. Unfortunately, there still seems to be many physicians that haven't been educated or have even heard about PFAPA. Therefore, you may be in a situation where you need to educate your doctor or search for one that is familiar with the condition. Armed with the information and personal stories in this book, you can be your child's advocate and talk to your doctor if you suspect your child has PFAPA.

PFAPA is typically apparent or diagnosed in children under the age of five. Usually by the age of 10, the child out grows the illness, though there have been reported cases of adults that continue to live with this affliction.[4]

In order to diagnose PFAPA, your doctor may need to rule out other diagnoses, meaning that a simple blood test or a throat culture is not enough to confirm a PFAPA diagnosis. This makes waiting for the ultimate diagnosis very frustrating for PFAPA parents because there are usually months or years involved before a diagnosis is finally pinpointed. It's also important that your doctor considers performing the appropriate laboratory testing to rule out other disorders, that if left untreated, may result in more severe medical issues.

As a PFAPA parent, it's extremely important for you to identify your child's symptoms as well as understand what to look for in order to communicate your findings to your doctor. Your doctor isn't with your child 24/7 and a typical office visit lasts about 15 minutes. You are your child's advocate and have the ultimate responsibility of communicating what you have been noticing about your child's recurring fevers. You should come prepared with details and information about what your child is experiencing, such as a fever log. Tracking detailed information on each episode may assist your child's doctor with the information needed to help solve that mysterious puzzle of diagnosis. Some of the common traits and facts for considering a PFAPA diagnosis include:

1) Sore throats are a complaint of many PFAPA diagnosed children. Throat cultures are typically negative, even though the child may appear to have enlarged or swollen tonsils. Having repeated throat cultures may be difficult for your child to endure, but is important in ruling out other diagnoses, such as tonsillitis.

2) One important exclusion test is the absence of upper respiratory infections.[5] Symptoms in PFAPA diagnosed children don't include any cold like symptoms that can be associated with a virus or cold. So, if your child is experiencing cold-like symptoms, chances are, the episode is a non-PFAPA episode.

3) PFAPA diagnosed children seem to be unusually healthy between episodes. Once their fever subsides, they are typically full of energy and vigor, just as though they never had a fever. Some parents have felt that their PFAPA diagnosed child is less likely to pick up other illnesses, including colds, due to the nature of their over active immune system, which is thought to be a trait of PFAPA patients.

4) Some PFAPA diagnosed children suffer with joint pain and/or mouth sores, both of which are very painful. These are not symptoms for all PFAPA diagnosed children, but in some cases, the mouth sores were a precursor, appearing ahead of a fever episode.

5) PFAPA diagnosed children tend to have normal development between episodes and there doesn't appear to be any research indicating that growth is stunted in any way.

6) The use of antibiotics does not assist in alleviating any of the PFAPA symptoms. Unfortunately, antibiotics are prescribed unnecessarily in many situations. The use of antibiotics, which may provide a false sense of security are in fact useless during true PFAPA episodes.

7) The use of acetaminophen and ibuprofen doesn't have a profound impact on reducing your child's fever between episodes, even if rotated on a schedule. This doesn't mean that the temperature won't decline some, but the drugs just don't seem to have an overwhelming improvement in the fever cycle.

8) The use of a single dose of Prednisone, as prescribed by a doctor, has the immediate impact of reducing your child's fever within one to three hours. Other drugs, such as Orapred, Cimetidine, Singulair, and Colchicine have also been used to treat PFAPA successfully. As with any prescription drug, your doctor should prescribe the drug and dosage. Not following instructed doses may result in an emergency situation. If you are unsure about the correct dosage, you can always contact your child's doctor's office or your local pharmacist. It's important to note that Prednisone has been known to relieve other periodic fever syndromes, so it is recommended that you talk with your doctor about the option of testing to rule out other diagnoses.

9) PFAPA fevers episodes tend to escalate quickly and in varying degrees of temperature. PFAPA is commonly associated with high temperatures, often above 103 degrees, though an episode can include any degree of fever-like temperatures. PFAPA episodes usually represent a quick fever ramp-up and a quick descending temperature when the episode is ending.

10) Many PFAPA diagnosed children have been known to have a drop in temperature about a day prior to fevering and some children may even complain of being cold or having a headache. Monitoring your child's temperature might be a way to track the onset of an episode.

As a parent, taking note of your child's symptoms may become the single most important information your doctor needs in helping to diagnose your child with PFAPA. The use of a fever log will become important evidence for your doctor to review during the episodes that aren't documented by a call or visit to your child's physician's office. As a parent, you may want to consider logging a call into your physician's office and speaking with a nurse so that the episode is noted in your child's medical chart. These documented episodes might be important in demonstrating the medical need for a tonsillectomy or T&A, if that is the route chosen by you and your child's doctor.

❖   ❖

Keeping a Fever Log

Starting a fever log will be a useful tool for you and your child's doctor to diagnose and treat your child. It will become your roadmap to understanding your child's symptoms and helping alleviate them as well as establishing a periodic time frame for fever occurrences. See the *Appendix* for a sample fever log to use at home in tracking your child's symptoms.

One important item to note is that although some families are able to predict the regularity of their child's fever, there is no set formula for a fever reliability time line. In Sierra's case, her fever could recur as often as every 21 days or she might skip a cycle and go two months without a fever. This is why the fever log is so important in establishing the periodic nature and individual symptoms of each fever episode. By noticing, acknowledging and logging the symptoms, you may also be able to differentiate the flu or other illnesses which may require a doctor visit, antibiotics or other prescribed drugs to treat the condition. The fever log will also be a good resource for your doctor in establishing an appropriate diagnosis, whether or not the diagnosis is PFAPA.

The fever log will also be an important piece of evidence if you are in the situation of having to educate your physician or convincing your Ear, Nose and Throat (ENT) doctor that;

1)   that there is a definite periodic nature to your child's fevers and,

2) you are opting for a tonsillectomy or a tonsillectomy and adenoidectomy (T&A) for your PFAPA diagnosed child.

Although a tonsillectomy or T&A is not the only treatment option for PFAPA, if being considered, it is likely your ENT will want to confirm that sore throats or enlarged tonsils have occurred several times during a year in order to justify the surgery. Unless you've logged an office visit with each fever episode, your fever log might provide substantiation of the periodicity of the fevers. ENT's will not just perform a surgery because you've asked them to. The doctor must be convinced the surgery is in the best interest of the child and that there is a valid medical reason to perform the surgery. You may also be in the situation of having to educate your ENT about PFAPA and the medical studies that have shown that a tonsillectomy and adenoidectomy may be a cure for your PFAPA diagnosed child.

Applications for tracking fevers and medicine dosages are starting to become more main stream. Here are a few suggested websites for phone applications that allow you to track dosage, timing and some symptoms for your fevering child. Keep in mind prior to ordering that there doesn't seem to be an application out there currently that is able to track the extensive information that should be logged with each fever episode.

http://www.soundtells.com/TemperatureTracker/index.html

http://iphone.wareseeker.com/fevermeds.app/42d63de0d8

Other fever syndromes

PFAPA is not the only fever syndrome in which children may be diagnosed. There are several other conditions in which periodic fevers may be a factor, but there are three that seem to stand out and can be initially confused with a PFAPA diagnosis:

1) FMF – Familial Mediterranean Fever
2) TRAPS – Tumor Necrosis Factor Receptor-Associated Periodic Fever Syndrome
3) HIDS – Hyperimmunoglobulinemia D with periodic fever syndrome.

There is no rule indicating you must subject your child to genetic testing or blood tests to rule out these fever syndromes, but in some cases, it might be helpful to correctly diagnose your child. Many PFAPA diagnosed children can be diagnosed without having to rule out these other syndromes due to the parents being able to identify and describe their child's fever episodes.

I've included a chart highlighting some of the differences between these fever syndromes and how they differentiate from PFAPA.[6] This information should be used as a summary table only and should not be considered inclusive of all information related to these syndromes. As with any medical condition, the diagnosis should be made by your child's physician. Hopefully, this chart will be helpful for you as a parent, in understanding the differences between these fever syndromes, from a non-medical perspective.

	PFAPA	FMF	TRAPS	HIDS
Episodes	2 – 6 days	1 – 3 days	1 -2 days to weeks at a time	3 – 7 days with 1-2 month intervals
Typical Symptoms	Fever, mouth sores, inflamed tonsils or lymph nodes, joint pain	Fever, severe abdominal pain, pleurisy (infection surrounding lungs), joint disorders, rash on ankle or foot	Fever, abdominal pain, pleurisy (infection surrounding lungs), eyelid swelling, rash or skin lesions, scrotal pain, diarrhea / constipation	High spiking fever, chills, abdominal pain, vomiting, diarrhea, headache.
Methods of Diagnosis	Exclusion of other diagnoses, establishing recurrent nature of fever	Blood test / DNA testing	DNA testing	DNA testing
Common Treatment	Prednisone therapy, Cimetidine, Singulair, Colchicine, Tonsillectomy or T&A. Growing out of the illness.	Daily oral Colchicine	High dose Corticosteroids	Unknown

Some children may initially get diagnosed with PFAPA, and upon further testing, receive a different diagnosis. Talk to your child's doctor about what symptoms your child may be experiencing at home and about your gut feeling in regards to the diagnosis. You are your child's advocate and chances are the information that you provide to your child's doctor might be the information needed to solve the puzzle.

3. Personal Stories

Sierra's Story
Tigard, Oregon

It was October 22, 2001, when Sierra first entered the world. I labored all night, got up in the morning, helped my first daughter Shelby, then a month shy of her second birthday, get ready for daycare in between extremely painful contractions. I managed to not let her see my face squint in pain as I got Shelby ready, trying to make her laugh and smile as we sang songs, just as we did each morning. Shelby, my eldest, is one of the most loving, giving and happy children I know. I've nicknamed her my "Angel Girl".

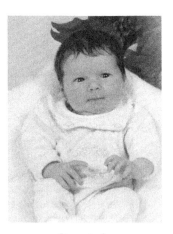

Sierra Amber

I made my way over to our car and my husband loaded up Shelby in her car seat and we drove to the daycare and dropped her off almost as soon as the doors opened, then rapidly headed for the hospital. I knew as I sat in the car, cringing as each contraction hit, that today would be the day when my second little angel would enter the world. I contemplated the prior week's events, almost in a daze, as we raced for the hospital.

With my first pregnancy, I had signs of toxemia and was induced a week early. Shelby was born at 9 lbs, 12 ½ ounces. Coming from a gene pool of relatively large babies and with a small 5'2 frame, my doctor had recommended and scheduled me for an induction the week before Sierra was due. After starting the pitocin on the day of my scheduled induction, I labored all day in the hospital and suffered through painful contractions. My doctor made the unfortunate announcement that the induction wasn't working, I wasn't dilating and I needed to head home and let nature take its course. It was then I suspected that my newest little angel, Sierra, would do things on her own terms.

Now, a week and a half later, as we headed for the hospital on the day Sierra was to be born, the labor pains grew immensely worse. It was all I could do to make what felt like a mile trek to the labor and delivery entrance, to actually walk across the parking lot. When I made my grand entrance through the hospital doors, my husband ran over to announce to one of the nurses that I was in labor. I fully expected to receive the movie star treatment: greeted with a wheel chair, being comforted by the staff asking me if I wanted ice chips and being led to my very own homey room. Instead, the nurse directed me to a temporary room and started to lecture me about false alarms. I'm not a yeller or screamer, but I quickly made my point and was admitted to the hospital within minutes. I was already at 7 centimeters and when contracting, was at 10 centimeters. This was no time to delay and I kept inquiring about the arrival of my very important anesthesiologist to administer some much needed relief. I had to beg like never before, since technically by the time I received my epidural, I was already at 8 centimeters. But, my pleas were granted and soon I was feeling great, dreamy relief. I personally commend all of the mothers that give birth the natural way, but that path just wasn't meant for me.

Approximately 90 minutes after I first entered the hospital, at 8:58 a.m., my newest little angel, Sierra Amber entered the world at 8 lbs, 13 ounces. She seemed so tiny compared to Shelby. I held her on my chest in disbelief at this newest little miracle. I cried tears of pure joy and happiness and all in the world was good.

Sierra was such a cheery little baby. She rarely cried, slept very well for a newborn, was a good eater, and really just an overall, precious little girl. She loved to cuddle, so I nicknamed her my "Cuddle Bug." It wasn't long before she started flashing her first smiles. My two little, beautiful girls made my life seem absolutely perfect.

Shelby and Sierra

Sierra joined Shelby at daycare when she was just three months old. She seemed to adjust well and was surrounded by people who genuinely loved her and cared for her. I wasn't surprised at all when she got her first fever on February 18th, 2002, at four months old. After all, she was in daycare and more susceptible to germs. I did nurse her however, and had hoped that the antibodies that she received through nursing would additionally protect her from getting sick. Shelby had been nursed too, and she had off and on colds since she had started daycare and from everything I had read, I just assumed this was one of the downfalls of daycare. I've always been a cautious Mom, so I did what any concerned Mom would do when their four month old has a fever, I took her to see our family practitioner.

Her first visit in February was followed by another visit, one and a half months later, on April 1st, 2002. I was beginning to question our decision to keep the girls in daycare, but financially, we really didn't have many options. Sierra quickly developed the same issues her sister had with ear infections, which ultimately led to a set of tubes being put in during 2002 by our ENT (Ear, Nose and Throat) doctor. All of this seemed normal to me. When Sierra's second set of tubes was put in during 2003, her problem with her ears seemed to resolve, but what didn't was her fevers. The difference with Sierra's ear problems from her sister's was that the symptoms weren't just fluid behind the ears and an occasional ear infection; with each preceding doctor's visit, Sierra seemed to have high fevers. Looking back, the fluid behind the ears and the ensuing ear infection diagnosis ultimately disguised her fevers. This seemed to puzzle her doctor and the nurses because there was fluid behind her ears at times and there weren't many ear infections once the tubes were in, but there always seemed to be fevers. Sierra was treated with multiple doses of antibiotics in her first two years of life.

2003 was a challenging year. My marriage started to fall apart and Sierra seemed to be sick all the time.

Shelby consoling Sierra during a fever episode during a 4th of July parade in 2003.

Both my husband and I worked outside of the home and we tried to share sick days so that we could take care of Sierra. My husband co-owned his own company, but for me, it became a struggle at work to justify all the time off, especially when I wasn't able to give my employer any notice on Sierra's sick days. Additionally, the rules at our day care didn't allow Sierra to come back to day care until she had gone

24 hours without a temperature. This automatically extended our sick days at home.

It got to the point that I could just call her doctor when she got a fever and sometimes we would go into the office for a check-up and other times not. Not knowing what we were dealing with at the time, I've relied on her medical file to document the following dates during 2003 in which there was an actual doctor visit due to those illusive fevers:

2003 Doctor Visits
5/28/03
8/18/03
9/9/03
11/11/03
12/2/03

Being an optimist by nature, I hoped that Sierra was just more susceptible to getting sick at daycare and maybe her immune system wasn't strong enough to fight these viruses. At most office visits, Sierra's doctor or nurse practitioner wanted to rule out strep. This meant Sierra was subject to the 'stick' as she coined it. It was a battle at the doctor's office trying to get Sierra to take her strep test, which usually ended with both of us in tears. Sierra is a strong willed, petite, little girl. When you look at her, she has an air of innocence with porcelain, doll-like features. When it was time for the 'stick', it would take three of us to hold her down while the doctor or nurse worked to get a swab from her throat. Sierra's screaming could be heard throughout the entire doctor's office and afterwards, she would fall limp in my arms, worn out from the fight and the fever.

With each strep test, her results were clear. The only symptoms she continued to display were a high fever and a slightly inflamed throat. There weren't any signs of throat infection and there weren't any other noticeable symptoms with Sierra, or any that she could communicate at her age, but her fever usually lasted for 1-4 days and then she was fine and back to her energetic self. Her treatment usually consisted of alternating doses of Tylenol and Motrin, which seemed, at times, to reduce her fever, but was never usually effective for very long.

Towards the end of 2003, I was in our doctor's office, during one of Sierra's unrelenting fever episodes and at my wits end, virtually in tears. I pleaded with Sierra's doctor, Dr. Joyce Endo, to tell me what was wrong with my daughter. I told her that Sierra now expected to get sick. My 'Cuddle Bug' was starting to think getting sick was just a part of her life. It grieved me to see her suffering like this. It was at that point that Dr. Endo suggested that Sierra see a Pediatric Infectious Disease specialist. I wasn't sure if I wanted to cry harder, thinking that Sierra could have some abnormal disease, or be happy that perhaps we were moving closer to figuring out what was wrong. I was afraid of what the doctor would say. Did my daughter have some sort of genetic problem, was it cancer, or a tumor? My mind just wandered as I headed out of the office that day. I immediately called and scheduled her appointment.

During the beginning of 2004, it was apparent my marriage was over. As the girl's Dad and I separated houses, we developed a joint custody visitation schedule so that we could each have equal time with Shelby and Sierra. We all worked to transition to our new life, including taking care of Sierra during her fever episodes. It was soon after this that it was time for our appointment with Dr. John Paisley, our Pediatric Infectious Disease Doctor at Legacy Emanuel Hospital and Health Center in Portland, Oregon and a highly respected physician in the area. I was both nervous and excited as we entered his office with Sierra in tow. I filled out a lengthy medical history, communicated Sierra's medical issues and answered the many questions that Dr. Paisley asked. I think it was primarily to rule out other diagnoses, but the questioning itself was rather intense and very thorough. He then examined Sierra.

After the examination, Dr. Paisley left the room for a while and when he returned, he had some medical literature. It was a journal article on PFAPA, which is short for "Periodic Fever, Aphtous Stomatitis, Pharyngitis and Adenopathy". My head was spinning. As I sat there, stunned, Dr. Paisley explained what PFAPA was and told us about different treatment options, such as prednisone and a tonsillectomy. There was so much information to digest.

He also mentioned that there was a support group for families with children diagnosed with PFAPA on Yahoo and suggested that we look into the group. Thoughts were racing through my mind as I tried to comprehend all of the information he was telling us. He prefaced his information by saying he wasn't 100% sure that PFAPA was what Sierra had, though he thought it was very likely and recommended that we begin keeping a fever log. He handed us a prescription for prednisone and suggested filling it the next time Sierra fevered. He informed us about the pros and cons of each alternative for dealing with PFAPA and communicated that Prednisone had been known to shorten the actual fever cycle, but to increase the frequency of onset. Knowing Prednisone was a steroid, I was immediately reluctant to try it.

That afternoon, my information quest began. I first tried Google. I searched for 'PFAPA' and 'Periodic Fever Syndrome' and all I found were a few journal articles on the medical aspects of PFAPA and most of them weren't written in layman's terms. Next, I searched Yahoo and found the PFAPA group administered by Fran Bulone. I filled out my necessary information and waited for her to accept me to the Yahoo PFAPA group. This group was a God send to me. It's hard to explain what I felt when I started reading the posts. My eyes watered and my heart seemed to skip a beat. I had found my virtual family. I was connecting with complete strangers who had many of the same questions that I did. Sierra fit the profile perfectly of many of the other children that were diagnosed with PFAPA.

Sierra's next fever occurred about 20 days after our visit with Dr. Paisley. I held on to the Prednisone prescription for some reason, reluctant to fill it. I was worried and concerned about the ramifications of Sierra taking a steroid. But, Sierra continued to fever like clockwork. Sometimes the fevers were up to 90 days apart and sometimes they occurred every month. I continued to keep a log of Sierra's fevers and symptoms, which proved to be difficult as she spent time between her two homes. I managed to record what information I could and was soon noticing a trend.

On March 10th, 2005, Sierra fevered again. I felt I had read enough online on the PFAPA support group and wanted to give the prednisone a try. I filled the prescription and gave Sierra her first dose. The taste was almost unbearable for her. It was hard enough getting her to take any medications, let alone an unflavored dose of steroids. Her gag reflex caused an immediate purge and she threw up even before swallowing the medicine. I waited a couple hours and we tried again. This time she reluctantly swallowed and we waited. Miraculously, within about 2 hours the fever dissipated and she began showing signs of energy and increased appetite. I had difficulty believing this was really true. She started the day with a fever of 103.4 and around 6:45 p.m. her fever was gone. I thought I had found her miracle drug, her cure.

Soon, my overwhelming happiness was crushed by another onset on March 22nd, 2005, just twelve days after I had given her the prednisone. Reluctant to give her another dose of Prednisone, I opted to let the fever run its course. That fever episode lasted three days.

Sierra fevered again on April 11th which was 20 days after her last fever. This fever seemed to take a real toll on Sierra. After leaving her doctor's office, I arranged to take the next day off of work and stay home with her, knowing that she had at least another day in her cycle. Early afternoon on April 12th, Sierra's fever spiked to 104.6. She was extremely cold and began shivering. I wrapped her up in blankets and tried to warm her. Her fever had never been this high before. Within minutes her lips seemed to turn an icy blue color and she started having what appeared to be mini seizures, later concluded to be a febrile seizure. I was in panic mode. I called her Doctor's office who directed me to immediately drive her to Emmanuel Children's Hospital, rather than the closest hospital. Emmanuel was only about 25 minutes away, but I'd never been to the actual hospital before and wasn't exactly sure where I was going.

I frantically loaded Sierra into her car seat and as we drove towards the hospital, she seemed to be gagging in between her seizure-like movements. I wasn't sure if I should pull the car over and call an ambulance or move forward on my mad quest towards the children's hospital. In sheer terror, I drove as fast and safely as I could, uncontrollably crying. My mascara had started to collect in my eyes causing burning and blurriness. I struggled to wipe my face and attempt to gain my composure as I called her Dad to meet me at the hospital.

When I arrived, Sierra was triaged and we were told to wait in the waiting room. Her seizures had stopped and she was just limp in my arms. We were soon moved to the pediatric waiting room and Sierra's fever seemed to stabilize around 101°. Once in the pediatric ER room, I tried to explain to the attending physician what had occurred and communicate to the doctor about Sierra's PFAPA diagnosis. The doctor had not heard of PFAPA, which was frustrating to me, especially at a children's hospital.

The attending physician recommended that an IV be initiated, since she was refusing to drink any liquids or suck on a popsicle, in order to rehydrate her depleted little system. I suggested that we may want to get an additional person or two to hold Sierra down if we were going to attempt to do this, knowing her fear of shots and her uncanny ability to resist restraint, similar to how she reacted with her regular strep tests at her doctor's office.  Rather than bringing in an additional person to help hold her down, the doctor opted to bring in a small, white, children's straight jacket that allowed for restraint of the upper body, but would permit an IV insertion on the top of her hand. I really didn't recognize what it was until they started dressing her with it over her hospital gown. She seemed fine at first and cooperated with the dressing until she realized what was happening. As the two nurses held her down, the doctor moved towards her to insert the IV. Sierra was screaming at the top of her lungs, kicking her legs and flailing about. Within seconds she managed to kick the doctor in the head and misalign her eyeglasses almost knocking them from her face. All this from a 4 year old, little, blue eyed girl who was lethargic and exhausted from her fever. Sierra has an unbreakable spirit. It brought me back to my pregnancy and the induction that didn't take because it wasn't on Sierra's time.

After three tries of the IV needle, the doctor gave up on the IV and asked Sierra to promise to drink liquids, which she did. I was thankful that the trauma was over. After a few more hours in the ER, we were told we could leave the hospital. Sierra's fever had stabilized to a low grade and she didn't have any additional symptoms. She was exhausted and slept as soon as she hit her car seat.

On May 4th, 2005, which was 23 days after the last onset and hospital visit, Sierra fevered again. Her fever cycles seemed to be showing some unbelievable regularity. It was then that Sierra received her second dose of Prednisone. Just like before, there were dramatic results with her fever diminishing almost instantly and having her back to her usual self. The resulting problem was that the frequency again increased and a new fever was back on May 20th only 16 days after her last fever. Three bouts of fevers in 39 days was more than any little person should have to endure.

A call into Dr. Paisley prompted the tonsillectomy discussion. I had done some more research and found that the surgery had been successful with other PFAPA diagnosed kids, but not all were fortunate enough to benefit from successful tonsillectomy results in relation to PFAPA. Her Dad and I needed to make a decision on whether or not to have the surgery. Unlike during the 1970's when the procedure was an overnight stay, knowing that Sierra could come home after the surgery and I could personally care for her, helped to ease the apprehension a little bit.

There are risks with any surgery. I began weighing the pros and cons in my mind. Having had my own tonsils out as a child, I felt that the procedure wasn't an extremely invasive one and if it could potentially help my daughter, I was in support and wanted to give it a try.

The first step was making another appointment with her primary care doctor, who had already consulted with Dr. Paisley. Although her doctor hadn't heard of PFAPA until Sierra's case, she was on board with Dr. Paisley's recommendation after reading some material on PFAPA. This decision prompted Sierra's doctor to refer her to the ENT doctor that originally did her ear tubes when she was younger. Sierra's ENT was skeptical of taking Sierra's tonsils out, also not having heard of PFAPA. After some convincing and knowing that this decision was being supported by her primary care doctor and Dr. Paisley, and seeing Sierra's history of unexplained fevers, negative strep tests, and her fever log, her ENT agreed to schedule the procedure.

The morning of August 2nd, 2005, Sierra's life and my life changed forever. Although we didn't realize it at the time and though we had a few hard weeks ahead of us, removing her tonsils proved to be the right decision for us.

As I waited for Sierra to be taken into surgery, my heart was racing. I fought back tears knowing my little four year-old was going into surgery. The nurse finally came to wheel her pediatric hospital bed to surgery and rather than take my scared little girl, sitting on the big bed all alone, she asked another nurse to wheel the bed and personally carried Sierra away to surgery. I waved goodbye as I blew a kiss to Sierra, turned my head and burst into tears. Fortunately, she didn't see me crying. I felt so alone and scared wondering if this was the right decision. Even today, though Sierra was not quite four years old, she remembers being at the hospital and the mask of smelly air that made her fall asleep, just prior to surgery.

Sierra was in the operating room about 20 minutes for the actual procedure and then rested in intensive care recovery for another hour before I could see her. She woke up from the surgery screaming and disoriented. I held her and could not seem to console her. The nurse handed her Dad and I a dose of Tylenol to administer. After 30 minutes of crying, Sierra fell asleep. She woke up an hour later and was calm. She complained that her throat hurt but was talking and in good spirits. I drove her home and tucked her into her cozy bed for some movie watching and more rest.

Later that night the pain continued and I gave her more Tylenol. She didn't sleep well. The worst part of the recovery came at day 3 and lasted for a few days. Her throat had a terrible smell, which the doctor warned about, as the tissue in her mouth began to heal. The pain she was experiencing was incredible.

In order to comfort her, Shelby and I made snow cones and gave her popsicles to suck on. Her diet during this time was terrible, and she was already a picky eater. I didn't care though, whatever provided her comfort and hydration, I was willing to do. We managed to get through it and within a couple weeks, Sierra was once again my happy "Cuddle Bug".

When I look back at Sierra's medical records, the trend seemed so obvious. I wonder if I had not kept a log, what the pattern would have shown, since it wasn't every time that Sierra went to the doctor when she had a fever. The log was the best evidence to demonstrate to both her primary care doctor and her ENT that there was indeed a pattern with her fevers. It's my belief that her fever log and documented office visits ultimately contributed to helping convince her ENT to take her tonsils out.

We were fortunate enough to have a great family practitioner, Dr. Joyce Endo, who listened to my plea and made the referral to Sierra's Infectious Disease doctor. We were also fortunate that Sierra's ENT supported the decision to perform a tonsillectomy and felt it would be in Sierra's best interest.

I wonder to this day how our lives would be if Sierra kept fevering. Sierra does remember back to the days she used to get sick, though thankfully, she doesn't 'anticipate' being sick like she used to. She refers to those days as "before her surgery", and now announces to people when they ask her about her fevers, that she's now healthy.

Sierra has been fever free since that surgery on August 2, 2005 and is now a healthy 9 year old, fever free for 5 years.

Emma's Story

Location: Johannesburg. South Africa.
Onset: Emma first showed symptoms of PFAPA at
               11 months of age.
Treatment: T&A with Coblation Method.
Outcome: Successful, no fever recurrence.

Our daughter Emma was born on July 26th, 1998. It is hard to say when the fever actually started as it took a while to see a pattern, but I would say at 11 months of age.

Looking back, I think the pattern started directly after her 2nd Prevenar vaccination. For a while I thought that the vaccination may have caused all this trouble, but I no longer believe that and have given our son, Alexander, who is now nine months old and healthy, the same vaccination.

Initially, we were told time and time again that it was a virus. Emma presented with no other symptoms at that time. Her fevers would spike as high as 41 Celsius (105.8 Fahrenheit) and she often vomited during fever spikes. I believe the vomiting was a symptom of the high fever rather than the PFAPA. We learned to alternate Empaped (acetaminophen, not marketed in the United States) suppositories and Voltaren (strong anti-inflammatory) suppositories. Emma would refuse to swallow medicine so suppositories also worked well because of the vomiting. Alternating the two, we managed to keep the fever stabilized.

The episodes were very tough on all of us, with Emma sleeping no more than 2 hours at a stretch and crying almost non-stop. She was clearly in a lot of pain, even when the fever was under control. After about five months of fevers, we no longer accepted the virus diagnosis and our pediatrician agreed and referred us to a pediatric rheumatologist. With her help, we tested to rule out cyclic neutropenia, HIDS and childhood rheumatism and got a PFAPA diagnosis. We started seeing some longer breaks between episodes, one 12-week and one 16-week break. We were then prescribed prelone syrup (prednisone, same dosage as the US brand Orapred) and began treatment. Initially, it would break the fever within an hour. Later it would take up to 3-4 hours, but it always eliminated the fever and it didn't come back until the next episode. Prelone syrup worked very well, but it brought the episodes closer together. We were back to monthly, sometimes three weekly fevers. Emma started to complain of joint pain in her right knee just before and during the episodes. We were not sure whether this was a new symptom or whether she simply hadn't been able to verbalize it sooner, due to her age.

In December 2007, Emma's baby brother Alexander was born. Emma had an episode while I was in the hospital and four episodes in the following six weeks. It was clear to us that the emotional stress of having a sibling brought on these extra episodes. It was exhausting having her sick while we had a newborn and although we used the prelone syrup every time, we did not feel comfortable with the amount of cortico-steroids she was now ingesting and permanent medication was never a long-term solution.

Following recent studies, a consultation with a wonderful ENT and numerous success stories on the Yahoo PFAPA-board, we scheduled her T&A for March 2008, at 32 months of age. The surgery went well. Although Emma never once had any throat involvement at all, and only two cases of tonsillitis in her life, her tonsils were 'rotten' and were subsequently diagnosed with 'chronic tonsillitis.' The ENT used the coblation method rather that the traditional cauterization, which made for an easier recovery. It took ten days and lots of pain killers to get back to normal, but all in all it was easier to handle than a PFAPA episode without prednisone.

It is now October 2008, seven months after the surgery, and we have not had another episode. Emma has had other infections (ear, cystitis, etc.), but she did not even get a raised temperature with any of them whereas she used to spike high temperatures with every cold and infection beforehand. Basically, I have not used a thermometer on her since the day of her surgery.

She has also had a growth spurt, eats and sleeps better and is a much more energetic, happy and confident child. She used to be pale whereas now she has rosy cheeks. Even if the fevers return today, having the T&A done was the best decision we have ever made for our daughter.

Randi's Story

Location: Sault Ste Marie, Michigan.
Onset: Randi first showed symptoms of PFAPA at 4 months of age.
Treatment: Ongoing doses of liquid Prednisone.
Outcome: Ongoing Prednisone usage has successfully worked to minimize fever at onset.

"Randi, are you okay?" That was the question that started a chain of events in our lives that would forever mark our hearts with the grim reality we did not want to face. My wife and I had our little girl in the winter of 2004 and were so blessed to finally have a child after many years together of multiple attempts at trying to get pregnant. We noticed at about four months old that Randi started to develop low grade fevers that never displayed any other symptoms besides the fever. We always assumed that the fevers were a result of early teething or perhaps a common childhood illness and administered Tylenol with favorable results, calming the fever and soothing her.

The day that started like many other days with the hustle and bustle of both parents working and a toddler consuming your every spare moment ended in the emergency room with questions no one could answer. My wife had gone to work and I was at home with Randi who had yet another low grade fever. She was around one at this time and by now, although unusual, the fevers were common place in our lives. I remember Randi sitting in her walker in front of the TV staring with a blank look on her face. The pile of unfolded towels on my lap fell to the floor as I quickly went to her, parental instinct knowing something was seriously wrong. I picked her up and asked her if she was OK only to have her head fall straight back, eyes rolling back into her head. I completely freaked out as any parent would, not knowing what was going on. She was totally limp in my arms and looked like she was dying in front of me when I realized she was burning hot.

I believe God stepped in then and smacked some sense into me so I could think enough to take care of her. I ran with her to the bathroom and threw the water on full blast in the shower and put her under the water. She began to cry and regain body control while I was crying and begging her to wake up. I was so traumatized by this that my wife said I sounded like a thirteen year old girl screaming when I called her to come home.

That night in the ER, the doctor ran a battery of tests only to say that she must have a virus and that it should just run its course. That was the beginning of a phrase that would plague our lives for the next year and a half. Randi's fevers began occurring very close together and getting extremely high. We used both Tylenol and Motrin, piggybacking them so there was no lapse in coverage. I remember one of my co-workers making the comment, "Is that kid is sick again?" I hate that memory and it will never leave me.

Our local Doctor is a wonderful instinctive man with great life skills and he worked diligently to find something that would explain these bizarre fevers. Every time Randi would get real bad, we had blood work done and found absolutely nothing other than an elevated white count and swollen lymph nodes in her neck. The doctor would say, "Maybe this time we'll find an ear infection or strep throat" only to find nothing again and again. An illness, to explain these fevers, would have at least let us know why they were happening.

Over the next several months the episodes became cyclical, coming every 14 days like clockwork. The fever would cripple her for 4-5 days causing stomach pain, leg pain, no appetite, weight loss and fatigue. The stress on my wife and I became unbearable, if you can imagine what it's like to watch your child suffer month after month with only a couple of weeks of good time in between the fevers.

The summer of 2006 was supposed to be a joyous occasion, with my wife ready to give birth to our twin boys. During the birth, one of the boys drowned in amniotic fluid which resulted in us being rushed to University of Michigan with a grim outlook for his survival. I recall being there in the middle of all this hell when Randi developed a fever right at the beginning of the hospital stay. I wanted to get in my truck and just drive south until the roads ran out.

While on our way home from MSU to get things in order, our local doctor called and said he wanted us to go to Children's Hospital in Grand Rapids, Michigan to a Pediatric Infectious Disease Specialist for Randi. He was at his wits end and needed to move us to better care to figure this out. Wow, the timing of this news, right in the midst of our caring for our son in critical care, it was as if my doctor had dropped a bomb. I was so scared to think that Randi might have Leukemia or cancer, that I literally shook from the inside out and felt like I was going to throw up every day. My son was saved after a long stay in the hospital in a drug induced coma and came home right before my trip to Grand Rapids with Randi.

Doctor Dahl, a Pediatric Infectious Disease Specialist ran the show in Grand Rapids, completing every test under the sun to rule out all the horrible stuff you can imagine that strikes children. PFAPA is a diagnosis of exclusion, so doctors must rule out the imitators before they can properly treat this disorder.

I recall the feeling I had when Dr. Dahl said she was almost certain she had PFAPA and that she would most likely outgrow it or resolve it with a tonsillectomy. After all this time and suffering my little baby girl endured, knowing it could soon be treated and we would be put back on the road to as normal life you could ask for, well you can imagine how close that doctor came to receiving one of the biggest kisses in her life. She explained what PFAPA was and what drugs usually stopped it in its tracks. The choice we made was liquid Prednisone at the onset of a fever. We give her .5 ml (teaspoon) at the first sign of a fever and within an hour and a half she is burning rubber through the house instead of burning up. The steroid has been reported to make fever cycles closer together, but with us the fevers were so close we didn't notice that.

My wife is truly an unsung hero, so many nights she was up all night long holding her, caressing her little head and singing "you are my sunshine" to calm her down while Randi didn't understand what was happening. Often times, my nightly ritual included washing the bedding she threw up on, the nausea a result of the Motrin.

Although Randi's PFAPA is not cured, I can say one thing with certainty: PFAPA has caused me to take stock of my life, time and time again, and I realize what really matters. Once, while holding my little angel, she looked up at me with her cherub face and said, "Don't worry Daddy, I'll be okay". To think that she was worried about me during her time of illness made me realize what a special little girl God gave us. Thank You God and thank you Randi; you've made me a better person.

Theo's Story

Location: Portland, Oregon.
Onset: From infancy.
Treatment: Naturopathic and holistic approach.
Outcome: Successful, no fever recurrence.

Theo fevered ever since he was an infant. We were told by our pediatrician, naturopathic doctor and midwife that it is normal for babies to have many high fevers and that it helped them in developing a healthy immune system. We had our own private theory; our boy was such an active little fellow, was never much interested in sleep and we just felt it was in his nature to be highly active until he basically dropped.

When Theo was a year old, we had his astrological birth chart read just for fun. We were surprised when this highly skilled astrologer said to us without knowing our predicament that our boy was not a sleeper, was very energetic and is someone who would have a lot of fevers.

Time passed. For the first few years the fevers seemed to come every 6-8 weeks. Once we ended up in the emergency room when the mercury hit 105.8. Doctors told us that some children just get a lot of fevers; some babies also fever a lot with every tooth. We let his body fight off the fever un-medicated up until it reached 103 degrees and when it was higher, we used Ibuprofen or Tylenol.

Between the ages of 4-5, we began to notice that the fevers really seemed to be settling into a regular cycle. I began to record the fevers and found that they came every 28 days. At the height of Theo's fever, he would usually vomit and have mouth sores. Those were his main symptoms besides the high fever. These episodes would last 3-5 days.

Finally, I just felt something was not right even though his pediatrician assured me that Theo was healthy. My uncle, a retired pediatrician, encouraged us to do more blood-work and began to help me with my research. Our midwife, also a naturopathic doctor, mentioned that perhaps Theo had a periodic fever syndrome. I searched the web and discovered PFAPA. I felt I was finally finding a description of what our son had been going through. I called my pediatrician and alerted her to my findings and she concurred. We did the blood work and she recommended us to Dr. John Paisley in Portland, Oregon, who works with infectious diseases and had many PFAPA cases. We confirmed PFAPA as a diagnosis, when Theo was five years old, on Thanksgiving weekend. We were instructed to give Prednisone at the onset of his next fever if his symptoms cleared up in hours we could assume PFAPA.

It was absolutely miraculous! We thought we had found the cure. We called it "magic medicine." The fevers, the stomach pain, joint pain, mouth sores, extreme weakness, all vanished. Dr. Paisley assured us that the amount of steroid was safe, but he also warned us that with many children, it shortens the time between their fever cycles.

Prednisone quickly lost its luster. Sometimes the fever would return a few days after and cycles would shorten to a couple of weeks. He also began to get sick more often. Previous to this, Theo never got sick, except for his 'special' fevers. We learned that prednisone compromises the immune system. So, suddenly Theo had sore throats, more colds and got his first ever ear infection. These illnesses then would trigger a PFAPA episode. We were terribly distressed. We didn't know what to do.

The stress and worry of having a sick child with an illness that no one really understands was very upsetting. Theo's moods were amazing. He always popped out of the fevers, kept his good nature and bounce in his step; however, it was a lot for that little body to go through so much each month. As soon as he would be feeling stronger again he would sink with another bout. Our family did not sleep for 5 days out of the month, Theo was missing school and someone had to stay home from work to care for him. It was trying for us all.

At the height of our distress a woman on the yahoo PFAPA string wrote of an alternative doctor in our area who was treating her son and they were having results. We were game for anything. We then connected

43

with Dr. Nao, a woman who calls herself a holistic chiropractor with a special interest in immune system issues. I was skeptical about meeting Dr. Nao, but also hopeful. I would try anything. She was confident and felt she could help him. Yet, she was also polarized against allopathic medicine. This troubled me. As someone who has benefited from both allopathic western medicine as well as naturopathic and Chinese medicine, I prefer practitioners who can work together. The distrust that each side has of the other keeps the patient in the middle and unsure of what to follow. I am so grateful to our pediatrician, Dr. Gopal, who understood this dilemma. She took time with me as I explained Dr. Nao's philosophy about PFAPA and asked for her opinion. To her credit, she remained interested and supportive and always willing to work together.

Dr. Nao's path began with more blood work. She read the results differently than an allopathic doctor would interpret. In my lay-person's understanding her approach was to find out what was triggering the autoimmune response and why it stayed high. Theo's body fights infections when they are not present, the level of anti-bodies stays high. The IGA anti-body is high. She was looking for what keeps the antibodies high, since PFAPA is not a virus or bacteria from the outside. So, she also looked at food as a possible irritant. Anti-bodies over time attack the intestinal lining. The gut then gets thinner over time and the anti-bodies go up.

In addition to blood work, Dr. Nao administered a test to check for allergies and sensitivities towards certain foods. The test showed that Theo is sensitive to Gluten. Eating gluten then irritates the system creating more anti-bodies. Her overall approach was to lower the anti-bodies and with that eliminate the internal inflammation cycle that occurs. Avoiding gluten is one factor to reduce the antibodies.

Additionally, Dr. Nao's approach was to strengthen Theo's immune system. Theo's test results showed he tested low for B12, B6 and Iron. He had some indicators that demonstrated he was slightly anemic. Theo's blood tests were: HCT, HGB, MCV, MCH, and SGPT. Dr. Nao ended up treating Theo for mild immune hemolytic anemia and giving the B12.

RDW test is the red blood cell distribution width, which shows there were not enough mature red blood cells. Theo's IGM was high and indicated the antibodies were attacking his red blood cells. Increased IGM showed that there was an autoimmune inflammation attacking the red blood cells and the gut. Theo's absorption of food was not as good as it could be. The IGA was increased and showed that it was an autoimmune response that attacked the gut.

Dr. Nao also was not happy with Theo's glucose levels. Dr. Nao's interpretation of the levels varied from other western doctors. She claimed Theo was insulin resistant, stating his glucose was 109; and the normal range is 85-100. The insulin issue is also seen in the tests for carbon dioxide, and anion gap.

This might be more information than the average person needs to know, but for us it was wonderful to at least speak to someone who actually had a theory and understanding about what was happening to our son. The following was our treatment approach to support Theo's immune system and reduce the anti-bodies that fought his own system:

1. For the first three months Theo took a homeopathic remedy (called the Immuhauser method) that Dr. Nao made from Theo's own saliva. The idea was to make him more immune to his own system, since PFAPA is a reaction against one's own system.
2. Theo took a daily immune system nutritional supplement called Clear Vite.
3. For a time he took B12, B6, and Iron.
4. We applied twice a day an anti-oxidant cream called Oxi-cell.
5. Theo stopped eating wheat. By doing this, we were eliminating the irritants that created more anti-bodies. We also eliminated refined sugar which compromises the immune system.

Theo also complained of a "yucky" taste in his mouth, even when he wasn't fevering. There was no foul smell (except when he would fever). It was so bad that he kept a toothbrush in kindergarten so he could brush his teeth. We told this to Dr. Nao, who did a zinc test on him. It is a simple test with a special kind of liquid zinc. If a person is zinc deficient, the liquid tastes like water; however, if the liquid tastes unpleasant this was a sign that the person is zinc deficient. Sure enough we discovered that Theo was zinc deficient. We gave him zinc and the "yucky" taste was gone. We learned that zinc is important in having a healthy immune system. We monitor zinc on and off.

Dr. Nao's treatment also included hands-on work, a chiropractic bodywork style, no cracking for Theo. She worked physically with him on lymph nodes, and other body areas to help support optimal immune function. We saw Dr. Nao once a month in the beginning, then every 5-6 weeks, now we see her every two months.

Dr. Nao told us it would take 2-3 months to begin to see results as we began to implement her suggestions. In two months time, Theo had an episode that was less severe and had no mouth sores. The next time he was due to fever would have been his sixth birthday, May 13th. We were a little anxious because we had planned a birthday party and hoped he would be well enough for it. That month he missed his first PFAPA episode. We were thrilled. He even had a dream about it that indicated to us that his body was healing and he would miss the fever that month. In June, the following month, Theo had his last PFAPA experience. The fever wasn't as strong and there weren't any mouth sores. The episode lasted three days.

After that episode, we began to count weeks; 12 weeks and no fever, 20 weeks, then 26 weeks. Each week was a miracle to us. Our family felt lighter and easier. Theo thrived, looked less pale, felt stronger. Today as I write this, it is the eve of Thanksgiving, two years after we first diagnosed PFAPA, and one year and five months since Theo has last fevered.

We still keep up on seeing Dr. Nao every two months. Theo still takes the nutritional immune system supplement. We are easier with sugar, but thankfully Theo really only likes it here and there. We found many alternatives. He occasionally eats wheat and so far so good. However, it is just as easy for him to eat spelt and other sugars that we still maintain much of the diet. As he gets older he will experiment and make those decisions himself. He was always a good sport with the diet limitations. He knew what it felt like to be so sick and that it would be a big payoff for him if he could be well. We brought special 'no wheat' and cane juice sugar sweetened cookies to birthday parties and school functions and he did just fine. He self-monitored and was truly involved and surprisingly mature around his self-care.

Our pediatrician, Dr. Gopal, has been supportive and also curious and open about our path with PFAPA. Indeed, like many doctors, she has learned a lot through her experience with us. I was so touched by her suggesting at different phases that we put off certain vaccines so we would not aggravate Theo's immune system. We feel she understood and has always been incredibly kind and compassionate and willing to go the extra mile for us.

Last month I called Dr. Paisley who I always considered such a kind and caring doctor. He always had made time to talk to me during the days when I was so panicked and upset. I told him about our journey and what had helped Theo. He was totally interested and asked for the name and number of Dr. Nao. I was delighted by his openness and I am glad he would think of using her as a resource for other families.

My hope is that our story can be helpful to others. The PFAPA yahoo string that we have both been a part of is heart-breaking. I would spend hours reading emails, trying to find information and mostly only found desperation and heartbreak. It was rare to find "good news." However, what always shone through in that correspondence is the heartfelt care that people had towards others suffering and going through the same experiences. It is with that spirit that I share Theo's story.

Landon's Story

Location: Mesa, Arizona.
Onset: From 10 months of age.
Treatment: T&A.
Outcome: Successful, no fever recurrence.

Landon's road to diagnosis was a long, painful journey. I am not exactly sure when Landon started fevering but it seems as if it's always been a part of our lives. When Landon was a baby he would get ear infections often, which was always accompanied by a fever. When he was 10 months old, our pediatrician at the time said if Landon had one more ear infection, he would have to see an ENT. The ear infections went away; we never had to look into ear tubes so we were extremely happy.

However, the fevers did not go away. I was literally at the pediatrician's office every two weeks. We were told if a fever lasted more than 3 days, he needed to be seen. The fourth day of the fever I would bring Landon in to the doctor's office. I was told over and over again that his sickness was related to a virus.

I have another son who is 3 years older than Landon and he was never sick. I would bring this up to the pediatrician and he would dismiss me. My breaking point was when Landon was 18 months old. We took a family trip to Disneyland and had to come home. We never made it into the Disney Park because Landon was running a fever. We sat in our hotel room for two days. It was terrible enough for Landon, but also for his brother, who was 4 at the time. I had been hyping Disneyland to him for a month.

I took Landon into the pediatrician and demanded he have blood work done. The doctor was so rude and so against it, but agreed because I would not back down. Of course when they drew the blood Landon was screaming and crying and my younger son was very upset. He said to me "mommy why are they doing that to Landon"? Before I could reply the doctor snapped back "because your mommy wants us to do this to him."

I was furious! We never saw that doctor again and to this day I still think of how dismissive he was and because of him, Landon's diagnosis was delayed. In the end, Landon's tests came back normal which was comforting, but not too satisfying because the fevers were still coming every other Friday.

We went to another pediatrician and he basically was more of the same old story. I started to do my own research on the internet, but didn't happen to come across PFAPA until later. I felt totally ignorant, just wanting to know what was wrong. When Landon was 3, we went to another pediatrician and this time someone listened. The doctor didn't look through me. He agreed it was not normal to fever every other Friday for 4 days. He agreed to do some blood work at the end of Landon's fever cycle and found that his sed rate (measures inflammatory activity in your body) was high. He referred us to a hematologist. The hematologist ran a battery of tests and concluded that Landon had PFAPA. We were so happy that finally someone recognized that our son had something. There was a reason to the madness.

Landon was prescribed Prednisone. We gave him the Prednisone at the onset of a fever and like a miracle his fever was gone and he was back to normal. We were overjoyed. The Prednisone allowed us some freedom. We could go on vacation and not worry about having a sick child. However, our love of Prednisone was short lived. After a few months on the steroid, we noticed Landon was getting fevers every 5-7 days instead of every 14 days. We did not like pumping him full of steroids, but what was worse: around the clock Motrin and Tylenol for 4 days or 1 dose of Prednisone? We were unsure.

Our world changed when we found the PFAPA Yahoo group. Finally, we were with people who could understand our pain. I think it's hard for people to relate to this syndrome unless you have been affected by it. Everyone in the PFAPA group knows. They know your fears as well as the lack of information out there. To me it felt like they were walking in our shoes. I have a wonderful, supportive family, but I still felt so alone. I hated watching my baby suffer in pain every two weeks; it was heart wrenching. With that said, I hated to complain because I know there are so many horrible diseases children suffer with and how can you complain about something that is supposed to be benign? I was thankful in a way that it was only PFAPA because I knew it could be worse. The Yahoo group was a Godsend and I now had a support system and so much information to digest.

I had read some success stories about removing the tonsils and adenoids. My husband and I discussed and decided surgery wasn't for us. I was honestly petrified at the thought of surgery no matter how routine. My biggest fear was that it was no guarantee. Now, looking back, that was my biggest crutch. We also thought Landon would be outgrowing PFAPA soon; he was 4 and 1/2 at this time. We were told by the doctor most kids outgrow it by 5 or 6 years of age. So we were being optimistic.

Time went on and the fevers kept coming. He would complain of leg pain and his lymph nodes would swell on one side of his neck and now I was more aware of the canker sores in his mouth. He would stop eating the day before the fever would hit, but always drank liquids even during the fever. He dealt with the pain so well. He was so quiet during an episode. He would lie on the couch and watch TV and didn't ask for a thing. I would cuddle him and that is all he wanted. He was always very easy to please. When Landon was feeling well, he was very active, almost bouncing off the walls active. It was sad to watch because it was like having two children in one. One child was so lively and ready to take on the world and the other so sick and weak.

In July of 2008, we decided to look into the T&A. I was so nervous but more nervous about the amount of drugs we were pumping into Landon's little, growing body. When I think of the amount of Tylenol and Motrin this boy has had it makes my stomach turn. We always had two bottles of each in the house; it was a regular on my shopping list.

Landon had his surgery on September 8th, 2008, and came through it like a champ. I think he was so used to pain that he was able to handle this better than most. Landon has been fever-free since the surgery. It has been life changing for our whole family.

Landon turned 5 on October 1st, and it was the first birthday he had where he didn't have a fever. He is now just a happier child in general and is so much more agreeable now. In the past, he could be difficult and most things were a battle. Now, I feel guilty because I realized he just didn't feel well and who wouldn't be cranky and argumentative when feeling crummy. Landon never wanted to walk, even when not fevering. He constantly complained of his legs hurting; we would take a stroller everywhere we went. Four weeks after his surgery, we went to the zoo. Landon walked the whole zoo and never once asked to be carried.

I will not say Landon is cured; I don't want to jinx ourselves. The break has been wonderful and I hope it lasts forever. I am thankful for everyday that passes without a fever. No matter what the future holds I will not regret our decision to do the surgery, it worked for us, even if just for a while.

As for tips for other parents dealing with this syndrome I have a few.

1) I found that Motrin was more effective then Tylenol in taking down the fever. I would give Motrin every six hours and give Tylenol about three to four hours after giving the Motrin, this seem to keep the fever manageable. Landon's fevers would get high around 104–105 degrees. The Motrin would bring down his temperature to 100 degrees. Tylenol was only good to get us through the hours that we could not give the Motrin yet. The Motrin seemed to wear off after 4 hours.

2) Prednisone was good because it removed the symptoms, but seemed like a temporary fix for us since it brought the fevers closer together. I would also recommend getting Orapred rather than Prednisone. Prednisone tastes horrible and getting it into Landon was next to impossible. Orapred is a dissolving tablet, I would put it in apple juice and it was much easier to administer.

3) My biggest piece of advice is to be very assertive with your doctors. It seems that many are not familiar with PFAPA and it may be up to

you to educate your doctor. Keep fever logs; go armed to your doctor with information.

PFAPA remains a mystery, as there are so many unanswered questions. I hope one day we will know what causes it and what cures it. For now I am hoping we found our cure. I am enjoying my healthy boys and pray it will always be this way. I always tell Landon he is the bravest boy I know. He has proven to me that mother's intuition is always right. I knew in my heart of hearts what Landon was going through was not normal and I am so glad I listened to my heart.

Cade's Story

Location: Waxahachie, Texas.
Onset: Cade first showed symptoms when he was a year old.
Treatment: T&A.
Outcome: Successful, no fever recurrence.

My name is Leanne and my husband and I have three children. Tiffany is 27 years old and is about to graduate with a Doctorate in Pharmacy. Alisha is 22 and is in dental hygiene school. And, to our surprise, we had a baby late in life. I was 41 at the time, and my husband 44 when our precious son, Caden Rush, entered the world.

When Tiffany was about 4 or 5 she ran high fevers periodically. I kept taking her to the doctor and they did run several blood tests, but never found anything. Of course she took a lot of antibiotics to no avail. One day my pediatrician told me and my husband to just take her on a vacation out of the state. So we did, and took her to Missouri. And to our surprise, the fevers stopped. Tiffany eventually did have her tonsils out, but she was in her twenties. She runs 5 miles usually every other day. She played softball in college with a scholarship. So I don't think it affected her that much. Alisha never had fevers like that.

Cade came along and was perfectly fine until the age of 1 and 1 1/2 when he began to fever every two weeks like clockwork. But, at that point, we had not caught on to the recurrent nature of the fevers. Eventually I did and I asked the doctor what was going on. She sent me to an immunologist and he thought Cade might have PFAPA. He asked us to go home and the next time he fevered to give him Prednisone. We did and it reduced the fevers, but Cade was very irritable and looked and felt just horrible. We went to church a few days later and when I looked at Cade and he looked so pale and had dark circles under his eyes. I felt so bad for him that we just got up and left.

I called the immunologist and went back for a follow-up and told the doctor that the steroid had reduced the fever immediately. He said the diagnosis was probably PFAPA. He told us we could continue with the steroid or consider a T&A. I asked him if it was his child what would he do, and he suggested we move forward with the T&A. Thankfully it worked. Cade had his tonsils out when he was 3 and he is 6 now and doing great. I will admit some days he complains that his feet or his legs hurt, but not to the point that he can't play. Cade's feet are sometimes hot too. Who knows why? We have been to a Rheumatologist and he was checked with a good report.

Cade plays all sports and feels great so far. We are so thankful that the surgery has done this for him. I still worry that it will come back. I hope and pray that it never will. It is a very hard thing that these little kids go through. The cycle is terrible, they feel sick, they don't eat, fever, then not sick, play, and the cycle continues. Gain a little weight, lose a lot of weight, gain, and lose. It was a nightmare rollercoaster. My wish is that other families would at least consider T&A for their children. I had mine out when I was 5 or 6 and so did my husband and we do fine without them. I think that is not the issue though, the issue is surgery itself is something to not be taken lightly. So you do have to consider the risks.

Shannon's Story

Location:	The Colony, Texas.
Onset:	Shannon experienced recurring fevers at 3 years of age.
Treatment:	None.
Outcome:	Successfully outgrew recurring fevers at age 10.

When Shannon was three weeks old, we flew to Houston from North Carolina to visit relatives. When we arrived, my nephew was very ill with a high fever. Within two days, Shannon had it and became very sick. We took her to the doctor who was extremely concerned about her and put her on antibiotics. She recovered beautifully.

By three years old, Shannon was experiencing fevers every six weeks or so. Because I'm a stay at home mom, it perhaps took me longer to realize that she was sick more often than she should be. I would take her to the doctor, and we would usually just wait it out. She was not put on antibiotics for these episodes. After awhile, I stopped taking her to the doctor, because I knew the fevers would go away on their own.

By four years old, Shannon was able to communicate with me about other symptoms occurring. These included: sores in the inside of her mouth, stomach cramping, lethargy, headache, and of course, the fever. The fevers were usually very high – around 104 degrees.

By five, in kindergarten, when Shannon started missing so much school, I really started to worry about what was going on. It became so much more obvious once attendance was being kept that she really was sick a lot!!! This started my search for a diagnosis.

We had a wonderful pediatrician, Dr. Hector Hidalgo (Plano, Texas), who worked with us to determine what was causing the fevers. He sent us to a gastroenterologist, a neurologist, an allergist, and an ear nose and throat doctor. No one could determine the cause. The ENT suggested we remove her adenoids that were quite enlarged. Shannon was in second grade and we scheduled the surgery. At this same time, her father and I asked the doctor to remove her tonsils but he refused, saying that there was no reason for them to come out.

The surgery went well and six weeks later Shannon's fever was back. By this time, the illness was completely predictable. Several days before the fever would strike, Shannon would feel generally "yucky" and irritable, and then the fever would strike. It would spike high the first day and the fever would make her vomit violently. By day two, we could see the mouth sores, and her headache would be bad and the stomach cramps were horrible. By third grade, her school was pressuring us about her absences and I began my internet research.

For a year, I researched and studied everything I could find on the internet about different illnesses, conditions, etc. I knew that Shannon was thriving between fevers and was doing well except for five days every six weeks when she was sick as a dog. After countless hours of searching, I found an article about PFAPA. I knew immediately that her symptoms fit the criteria.

I went back to Dr. Hidalgo and presented the information to him. He had never even heard of it before. He agreed that it fit perfectly with her symptoms and sent us to an allergy/immunologist who gave her the official diagnosis. His name is Dr. Robert Sugarman in Frisco, Texas. Dr. Sugarman had two other patients with PFAPA. Dr. Sugarman was the one that told me that Shannon would probably grow out of it. By this time she was nine years old and we were beginning to hear of some success with removing the tonsils. Because of her age, her dad and I decided to wait it out and see if the fevers would go away on its own.

From age nine on, her fevers weren't as high and her episodes were shorter in length, but still like clockwork occurring every six weeks.

Shannon turned eleven this past January 2009, and has been fever free for one year! They just disappeared! Dr. Sugarman said that sometimes the fevers come back during the teenage years, so we'll wait and see.

Once we had initially received a diagnosis, I searched online and found the PFAPA forum that all of us parents read like the bible. Our story is quite different from most on the forum. We did not subject Shannon to any scary or extensive testing. We chose not to give her any medication except for Tylenol and/or Ibuprofen. Because we knew she was thriving in every other way, I was not as freaked out about it as some. We never even treated her as a sick child. She was sick for a week every six weeks, but other than that she was completely normal and we treated her like that.

My advice to parents with PFAPA diagnosed children is to not get too freaked out. You can just treat your child with over the counter medications to make them more comfortable and do not have to use steroids and other medicines. I do believe the tonsillectomy may have worked earlier on, but since that wasn't known when Shannon was younger, we didn't know it was a viable option.

Perhaps Shannon's exposure to the virus when she was three weeks old could have played a part in this whole thing. Also, I supposedly had strep throat every six weeks or so until I had my tonsils out when I was six. After talking to my mom through all this, we've determined that maybe I had this as well when I was little. Then with further research through older family members, we found out that my mother was sick with fevers when she was very young too. Shannon's paternal great grandfather and her aunt, my sister, both had/have Crone's Disease and I suffer from immune system issues as well (microscopic colitis, fibromyalgia). So, in my opinion, I believe that PFAPA is partly due to a compromised immune system, which again takes me back to that very early illness.

Good luck to all that are going through this. My advice: don't freak out too much and don't treat your child like they're not normal. They are! In fact, they don't seem to get all of the other sicknesses that everyone else gets. They just get sick differently. Love and prayers to you all.

Sami's Story

Location:	Quincy, Illinois.
Onset:	Sami started experiencing recurring illness from the 1 year mark.
Treatment:	Tonsillectomy.
Outcome:	Successful, no fever recurrence.

I truly believe that our family has an amazing guardian angel. Over the years many friends have inquired, "Have you ever asked yourself, why? Why do all these things happen to your family?" I tell them, I have asked myself that very question, many times, but with a different meaning behind it. When I ask it, I am saying, "Why me? What did I ever do to be blessed with such incredible children? Why me? Why did my children survive and thrive, while others haven't." I would not wish anyone to have to go through the pain and stress that my family endured, but I do know that because of it, I have a stronger appreciation of my family, my friends, myself and especially my guardian angel. I think if you read our story, you will believe in guardian angels too.

To understand Sami's story, you really need to begin on the evening of December 15th, 1993. On this day my second daughter, Summer, was ready to leave the hospital. Although she was 5 weeks early, she was doing great. The doctors agreed that she could go home but, the only problem was that the nurse forgot to do the PKU test which is required for all babies. The doctor suggested that we go home, get a good night sleep, and just come back for her the next morning.

When I returned to the hospital the next morning, I was told that Summer had been transported to Children's Hospital in Cincinnati (just right down the street) that the nurse thought something was wrong and wanted her checked out by the doctors at that hospital. Summer was diagnosed with a severe case of NEC (Neonatal Infection and Necrotizing Enterocolitis). This is a bacterial infection that an infant can catch that destroys everything in its path. The doctor's described it as bacteria "eating her organs". It can kill an infant within hours.

Summer went through a 13-hour surgery when she was just 3 days old. The surgeon told us honestly that her chances were not good and that he had never had an infant survive surgery that had a case as severe as Summer's. He said that if she lived she would be in the hospital for many months and she would have lifelong problems, most likely she would never walk, never talk, and would have brain damage. I don't know if it was denial or faith, but I kept telling him she would be okay.

My daughter Summer was released from the hospital 10 weeks later. She is now in ninth grade, a cheerleader, tennis player, and currently in the top of her class. I've read that of all premature babies, 10% will get a form of NEC, of those that get it less than 1% will have as severe case as Summer's. Our pediatrician told us that of all the babies he has seen over 30 years she is the sickest baby that has lived – and to this day she has no side effects from it. It just "happened" that the nurse forgot to draw blood, that another nurse had a feeling that "something just wasn't right", the best doctor in the country was in Cincinnati and available to perform the surgery. Two years later this doctor told me that if he did not see the recovery with his own eyes, he would say it was 100% impossible. I just told him I believe in miracles and my guardian angel.

My second miracle happened just 18 months later. My oldest daughter, currently 5, came down with a case of scarlet fever. After a very scary week with very high fevers, I thought we were past it. Then she started to complain that her leg hurt. I took her to the doctor and they could not find anything wrong with her. The next day it still hurt and she would not walk on it, so I took her to Children's Hospital emergency room. They said that nothing was wrong with it, that maybe she was just trying to get attention and just to give it a few days. The next day she was asleep on the couch and I bumped her leg and she woke up screaming. I took her to the emergency room again and told them that we were not leaving until they figured it out. The doctors were baffled and finally, at the encouragement of our pediatrician, ran a few tests. It ended up that the infection settled in her hip bone and it was quite serious. She was immediately started on several antibiotics and was released five days later. The doctors told us that she had a chance of developing Juvenile Arthritis and while researching this I came across another individual with the same thing that the doctors did not diagnose for over 3 months; this child ended up in a wheel chair.

Several years later we moved from Cincinnati to Washington, DC. As I presented "The Book", also known as 'our medical records', to our new pediatrician, he asked me if I knew how rare this was. He also asked me if Sunshine could walk okay, I told him she was a competitive gymnast. He said the odds of that are even greater than the odds of her having this in the first place. Thank you again Guardian Angel.

Sami is the forth of my five girls. She has always been the most caring, sweet child. We moved to Illinois when she was just 2 months old to be closer to my mom. Sami was born on my mom's birthday, so they always shared a special bond. Although my mom passed this last year, I am so thankful that she lived long enough to see the "new" Sami. Let me tell you about the "old" Sami…

I started to notice when Sami was around a year old that she seemed to be sick a lot. I mentioned this to her pediatrician and he said, "What do you expect with three older sisters bringing germs home." I don't think she gets sick anymore than most. Soon after that, he retired and we started to see another pediatrician, again I expressed my concerns. We were always at the doctor with Sami. Each time our issues were dismissed. I lost count of the number of times I have heard, "kids get sick, it's just another virus." I was finally tired of hearing it and went to another pediatrician. Sami still continued to get sick, and I continued to get told, it's just another virus.

When Sami was 5 years old, I got a huge wake up call. After being so angry that no one would take me seriously, I got out her insurance records and noticed that we had been at the pediatrician at least once a month for 18 months. That is as far as the records went back. I made an appointment with the pediatrician that very day. After showing her the records and telling her I know kids don't get sick that often, I have three others, she agreed to refer Sami to Children's Hospital to see an immunologist. Even so, I remember her adding, "If it will make you happy".

A few days later while we were visiting my mom, Sami came down with a terrible episode, she had a high fever, she wouldn't walk and she just looked lifeless. I was scared and the doctor would not call me back. I finally got a hold of the nurse and was told that it would be another 3-6 months before Sami would be seen by Children's Hospital. I was so upset and didn't know what to do. I remember asking my mom what she would do and she told me that the doctor had hundreds of patients, but Sami only had one mom and if I wouldn't fight for her, who was going to? This statement gave me the courage that I needed.

At that point, I called the doctor's office back and refused to get off the phone until I had a chance to speak directly to the doctor. I told the doctor I was taking Sami to Children's Hospital and to forward her records. The doctor told me that was completely unnecessary and I was over reacting. That was the last time I ever spoke to the doctor. At this point, her fever was 104 degrees, so I gave her a double dose of Tylenol and drove the 100 miles to the hospital. I prayed the whole way, for Sami, and that I wouldn't get there to just to be told I was crazy.

At Children's Hospital they listened, they looked at my journal and they finally believed me. It still brings tears to my eyes when I think of one doctor taking my hands and telling me, "We don't know what is wrong with your daughter, but we know something is wrong and together we will find out." What a relief, someone was listening and believing.

They kept Sami at the hospital for four days. She was so brave during that time. She was just so tired of being sick, that she just wanted to get better. They tested for everything they could think of, they said that some of the things that they were testing for were rarer than her just getting a virus every 26 days for three years. They thought she had FMF. They did genetic testing and then sent us home to wait for two long months. I remember calling my sister-in-law nurse and telling her that they thought it was FMF, but it was so rare that they said it probably couldn't be that. She said somewhat jokingly, "it's one of your kids, so that's probably what she has."

Sami still got sick, every 26 days she would get leg cramps and fevers and terrible canker sores in her mouth. Every month I could only sit and hold her and cry and pray with her. She would be sick for around 5 days, but it would take a good week to 10 days to get her energy back. She used to come up to me the day before and say the sickness was coming. I was always amazed how she could tell. It was hard on our whole family, life couldn't stop for everyone because Sami was sick; there was still soccer games, gym meets, our jobs, the list went on. We got to the point that we would just wrap her in a blanket and take her with us. My husband and older daughters and I would rotate taking days off with her. Yes, we got some looks. Why are you taking such a sick kid out, but we had to do what we could to take care of our family. We got used to the looks, even when we would turn down a birthday party for her a week beforehand, because we knew she would be sick. I'm sure some people thought we were crazy. We found it really didn't help to explain. This was so crazy, that if it wasn't happening to me, I don't think I would even believe it.

I researched day and night to find anything I could find that was even close to an answer. Finally I found an article on PFAPA, or Marshall's syndrome, and I knew that was it. I couldn't wait for our appointment at Children's Hospital. Armed with article and article about PFAPA, I was ready to take on the doctor, the hospital, the world if I had to. The wonderful thing was I didn't have to. The doctor agreed that she had PFAPA, but he also said something else was going on with her. Her strep level kept rising in her body. At the hospital it was 200, a normal level was around 140, and now it was over 400. They sent us home with Prednisone for the next episode, and the doctor said that if the symptoms stopped then she most likely did have PFAPA.

The next episode we gave her the Prednisone and could not believe that her symptoms all went away within a few hours. We thought this was the best thing. Unfortunately, our happiness was short lasted. She had another episode a week later and again we gave her the medicine. It did the same thing, but then she was sick three days later. The main problem we had with the medicine was that it would turn her into a monster. One teaspoon made a total transformation from a sweet child to just pure evil. After the second dose, my husband and I agreed we would not give it again.

We continued to go back to Children's Hospital monthly for the next six months, during this time her strep level just kept increasing; 550, 700, 900, 1400, 2700, and 5200. I could see the worry on the doctor's faces and I was getting scared. The doctors were baffled, and said that with levels like that she should be in the hospital and not even able to get out of bed. The doctors tried everything; they talked to other doctors throughout the country, they researched and researched. Even though I knew they didn't have answers, I kept calling and hoping. I told him once that I knew he was tired of me calling, but I had to do everything I could. He told me that if it was his daughter he would be doing the same thing. He said they just were running out of options. I told him about the study in Israel about removing the tonsils and said that is what I wanted to do. He said he didn't recommend it, but had no alternative plans.

We got an appointment that week to see a specialist and he was wonderful. He said he had no reason to think it would work, but I believed in it and he knew we were running out of time. He finally said, "Why Not? We'll do it!" Her surgery was one month later. She spent five days in the hospital and it was a rough surgery, but it was also the end of the "old" Sami.

It has been two years with the new Sami. She is thriving in school in activities. She has friends and play-dates and birthday parties and she is just so happy. For some reason she still gets canker sores, but her strep levels are normal again. I know that the PFAPA can return at anytime, I pray every night that it doesn't. But I also know that, somewhere out there, she has a guardian angel watching over her and she'll be okay.

4. PFAPA Treatment Options

What type of Doctor should your child see?

The individual doctor may be more important than the specialty; however, many PFAPA diagnosed children end up being diagnosed by a Pediatric Infectious Disease doctor. Immunologists and Rheumatologists are often specialties of doctors that are familiar with PFAPA and knowledgeable enough to treat PFAPA diagnosed children or recommend the necessary tests to rule out other fever disorders. It's a good idea to interview any potential doctors and ask questions about their knowledge of PFAPA. Knowing that your child's potential doctor is knowledgeable and familiar with PFAPA may help to eliminate unnecessary discussions and tests that your child may be subject to.

❖   ❖

Options for PFAPA Management

Your child's doctor will discuss some PFAPA treatment options with you. Unfortunately, there are no clear cut solutions to cure PFAPA, so it's important to fully understand the treatment options available as well as the side effects to make sure that you are in agreement with your child's prescribed treatment plan. There are a few treatment options that have helped to either alleviate symptoms or completely cure PFAPA diagnosed children. As with any plan of treatment, you should consult your child's doctor prior to administration of any medication to ensure the appropriateness and proper dosage of the drug. Some of the common treatment options include:

1) Prednisone
2) Orapred
3) Cimetidine
4) Singulair
5) Colchicine
6) Tonsillectomy or T&A
7) Waiting for your child to outgrow PFAPA
8) Alternative approaches for dealing with PFAPA

Several of these medicines have a distasteful flavor. Make sure to ask your pharmacist about flavoring options, if available.

❖   ❖

Prednisone

Prednisone is a steroid that has been known in many PFAPA cases to immediately reduce the PFAPA diagnosed child's fever to the point of completely resolving the fever within a matter of hours. Its unusual effects of immediate fever reduction on the PFAPA diagnosed child have been a wondrous assistance for many PFAPA families. The steroid, given in small doses, which may be flavored on request to make it more appealing for your child, also seem to have the side effect of increasing the frequency of fever episodes in some PFAPA diagnosed children. According to www.drugs.com, Prednisone prevents the release of substances in the body that cause inflammation. The drug is commonly used to treat arthritis, skin conditions, lupus, psoriasis, allergic and breathing disorders.

One of the side effects of Prednisone is linked to weakening immune systems. It is not known how this side effect may affect PFAPA diagnosed children. However, it is important to be fairly certain that your child is having a true PFAPA episode before administering the Prednisone. If your child is experiencing another type of illness, such as a bacterial or viral condition, administering Prednisone may complicate your child's immune system. Another side effect experienced by some PFAPA diagnosed children is aggression. Some families have reported additional characteristics such as hitting, being moody, clingy, hyper, angry and being loud as other behaviors demonstrated while taking this medication. This does not seem to affect all children and these behaviors seem to be more commonly found when giving PFAPA diagnosed children multiple or larger doses. It's important to make sure your child is getting enough calcium in their system if there is prolonged use of Prednisone. Prednisone is a generic, so the over-the-counter cost is less expensive than some of the other options.

Orapred

The generic of Orapred is Prednisolone, which is essentially the same medicine as Prednisone. The makers of Orapred developed a good way to hide the taste of the steroid. It can be expensive, but it is typically only used once per spell. According to www.about.com, Orapred is a corticosteroid and used to treat swelling, redness, itching and allergic reactions of the eye. Orapred is part of the steroid family and is used to prevent the release of substances in the body that cause inflammation, similar to Prednisone. Orapred seems to have the same effect on PFAPA diagnosed children that Prednisone does, though Prednisone seems to be more commonly administered to PFAPA diagnosed children. There have been several cases referenced on the Yahoo PFAPA support group of Orapred working extremely well in the treatment of PFAPA. Some doctors suggest that the continued use of Prednisone and Orapred will eventually end up spacing out your child's fevers, rather than increasing the frequency. There is no medical information to date that supports this claim; however, it has seemed to work for some PFAPA diagnosed children.

Cimetidine

Cimetidine is commonly used for the treatment of ulcers, active gastric ulcers, gastroesophageal reflux disease (GERD), heartburn and the prevention of gastrointestinal bleeding according to www.medicinenet.com. Some doctors recommend the use of Cimetidine for PFAPA diagnosed children, which may help to relieve some of the stomach pain and mouth ulcers experienced by children. The most common brand name of this drug is Tagamet. Tagamet is commonly used to treat heartburn and acid indigestion, but has been successful in the treatment of PFAPA diagnosed children. Some parents who use Cimetidine for their children have seen wonderful results with increased appetite and a reduction in fevers or even stopping fevers all together. The success rate with Cimetidine seems smaller with PFAPA cases then with the use of a steroid or a T&A, but it does work extremely well for some children.

Singulair

Singulair is used as a long-term (maintenance) treatment to prevent or treat asthma, allergies or hay fever, according to www.webmd.com. The drug works by blocking certain substances (leukotrienes) in the body. This effect helps to decrease symptoms (e.g., breathing problems, sneezing, stuffy/runny/itchy nose) caused by asthma or allergies. Although not as common as Prednisone, this drug has been prescribed successfully in some PFAPA cases to reduce or even cease PFAPA symptoms all together.

Colchicine

Colchicine is primarily used for treating gouty arthritis and to prevent acute attacks. According to www.medicinenet.com, this drug is also used to treat FMV (Familial Mediterranean Fever) patients. Colchicine is not as common as Prednisone in PFAPA cases, but has been prescribed to treat PFAPA diagnosed children.

Tonsillectomy or Tonsillectomy and Adenoidectomy (T&A)

Interestingly, there have been several studies, many of which are available online and some of which are referenced in the *Appendix*, showing the cure of PFAPA in children that undergo the tonsillectomy or T&A. The most encouraging study is one headed by Dr. Licameli which shows a 96% success rate in PFAPA diagnosed children that have undergone the surgery. Although, it's important to acknowledge that this procedure is not an absolute cure, nor should this procedure be taken lightly. There have been some children that have under gone the surgery with little or no improvement.

This procedure removes the tonsils or both the tonsils and adenoids under a general anesthetic and typically as an out-patient procedure. Depending upon the physician and the age of your child, some PFAPA diagnosed children may require an overnight stay at the hospital.

The most common and traditional method for tonsil and adenoid removal involves a surgical removal and cauterization of the affected area. There is an alternate method used by some ENT's referred to as the Coblation method, which was cleared by the U.S. Food and Drug Administration in 2001 and is trademarked by ArthroCare. This method, according to answers.com, uses radiofrequency, via a Coblation wand, to dissolve the affected tissue, while causing very little harm to the surrounding tissue. Many PFAPA parents report that this procedure eases the recovery time and pain involved in the traditional method.

With Sierra, the thought of her undergoing the knife just terrified me. But, after months of fevers, trying Prednisone and knowing that she would most likely continue with fevers after she entered the school system, I felt that the tonsillectomy was the best option. I did my own research and found that in many PFAPA cases, the children were cured. After discussing the risks with Sierra's doctor, her surgery was scheduled. Sierra underwent the traditional tonsillectomy method. I am still unsure as to why my ENT opted for only a tonsillectomy as opposed to a T&A, but the tonsillectomy did work for Sierra. The Coblation method was never brought up as an option by Sierra's doctor and I was unfamiliar with it at the time. Many of the PFAPA studies includes cases of children that have a T&A and the success rate with that option; however, there are many posts on the Yahoo PFAPA support group site that include children that just have their tonsils removed with a similar success rate.

Waiting for your child to outgrow PFAPA

Many parents, not wanting to opt for an evasive surgery or administering optional drugs, opt to wait for their child to outgrow PFAPA. In many cases, the PFAPA diagnosed child outgrows their symptoms by approximately age 10 or in some cases during their teen years. Although some parents may not want to wait through the many months of fevers, this is a valid and safe option for those families wanting to let nature take its course. Waiting is also not a 100% sure PFAPA cure as there have been known cases of adults having PFAPA symptoms and never growing out of the illness.

❖   ❖

Alternative approaches for dealing with PFAPA

There is a separate PFAPA Yahoo group dedicated to alternative approaches for treating PFAPA diagnosed children. That site is: http://groups.yahoo.com/group/PFAPA Alternative. Within this book, Theo's story is about a family with a PFAPA diagnosed child that turned to alternative approaches to helping their child cope, which in their case, has been successful. At present, there is not much research available for those families wanting to research an alternative treatment for their PFAPA diagnosed child. By signing up as a member on the PFAPA alternative website, you can search parent posts to see what alternatives are available.

5. Helping your PFAPA diagnosed child cope

Being sick every month is no fun, especially for a young child who is full of energy and doesn't understand why sickness is a part of his or her life. By helping your child to cope with their periodic illness, it will help you to deal with the stress of caring for your sick child.

In Sierra's case, she was too young to understand why she was constantly sick. She would explain to people that she got sick regularly and she'd talk about her sickness as a way of life. As a Mom, I was devastated hearing her explain to people that she was always sick. As if dealing with PFAPA wasn't hard enough, it broke my heart that my daughter just expected to get sick. In order to help her stress level and mine, we preemptively worked to manage people's expectations as well as organized our life to make it easier to deal with her illness.

❖   ❖

Educating the people in your PFAPA diagnosed child's life

Sierra was in daycare when she was first diagnosed with PFAPA. It's much easier academically to miss daycare rather than school, but it was difficult for me to miss so much time from work.

Your daycare or school may have rules or regulations which prevent your child from coming back into the environment within 24 hours of suffering from a fever. In some cases, some additional explanation or education may go a long way in helping your cause. Not only will their caregivers or teachers understand what PFAPA is, but may be able to bend the rules some in order for your non-contagious child to return to their day care or school environment.

Included in the *Appendix* of this book is a sample letter that can be given to your school or day care provider. It is recommended that you obtain a note from your child's doctor that indicates the PFAPA diagnosis and its non-contagious nature as well as include an article that discusses PFAPA. Give your daycare provider or your child's teacher time to digest the information. They may need to get approval to bend the rules to let your child return to the environment sooner than expected. More importantly, they will have a better understanding of what your child is dealing with on a recurring basis.

You may want to consult the Family Medical Leave Act for further information concerning time taken off work and whether or not your specific circumstances qualify: http://www.dol.gov/esa/whd/fmla/. Additionally, there is a website that is available that discusses special needs children and laws regarding their education. If PFAPA can be classified as a disability, you may find some helpful information at this website for dealing with their school system: http://wrightslaw.com/links/glossary.sped.legal.htm.

Dealing with the symptoms of PFAPA

There are several symptoms of PFAPA. It's smart to know about some of the options available to help soothe, if not eliminate some of the PFAPA side effects. The most common side effects include mouth sores, fever, joint pain, and sore throat pain.

Mouth sores or canker sores are a common symptom in PFAPA diagnosed children, but may not be present in all cases. While there is no way to prevent mouth sores, there are some things that may help with the frequency and the alleviation of the pain of mouth sores.

1) Vitamin L-Lysine – This vitamin has been unofficially shown to help with canker sores. It is an amino acid and works to reduce the frequency of mouth sores. Your child's doctor should be consulted to discuss the dosage and appropriateness of this natural remedy.

2) Numbing Agents – Orajel or other numbing agents may sting a bit when administered, but it does provide a numbing and soothing effect for mouth sores that are present and causing pain in your child's mouth.

3) Listerine – Twice daily regular use of Listerine or other mouthwashes have been shown to alleviate the frequency of mouth sores and in some cases, prevent them all together. Listerine is for adults, so if using on children, you may want to dilute the mouthwash or try another children's mouthwash. It's important to ensure that your little one does not swallow the mouthwash.

4) Toothpaste – There are toothpastes that are specially formulated to help reduce the frequency of canker sores. Sodium Lauryl Sulfate, which is commonly found in many types of toothpaste and some mouthwashes, may increase the frequency of canker sores by creating microscopic damage to the oral tissue inside your child's mouth. There are several toothpastes available without this ingredient.

5) Ibuprofen or Motrin – Use of ibuprofen or Motrin may help in reducing inflammation that is present surrounding the canker sore as well as the resulting pain.

For fever, sore throat and joint pain symptoms, I found it was easier to keep around a collection of items to have on hand when Sierra's fever struck. This became Sierra's 'Fever Reliever Box'. The contents can be edited to your child's specific needs.

'Fever Reliever Box' Contents:

1) Favorite washcloth or jelly cold pack – this is used to put on your child's forehead to relieve the fever. Dollar stores have great condensed washcloths that you can buy with varying designs that expand when immersed in water. Having a few of these in our box would offer Sierra a little excitement to find out what the design was before placing the cool washcloth on her forehead. Keeping kid designed cold packs in the refrigerator was something that I had on hand as well. Sometimes, it comforted her just to have something cool to press against her cheek.

2) Thermometer – find a thermometer that is easy to administer. Some of the ear thermometers don't work well with small ears. Find a good pediatric version and spend a little extra to get one that your child will respond to and will not fight when trying to take their temperature. This is especially important if you're trying to document your child's temperature on their fever log.

3) Over the counter medications –

a) Keeping Motrin and Tylenol on hand is helpful, even if it doesn't provide an extreme drop in your child's temperature. Rotating Motrin and Tylenol on a schedule seemed to at least keep Sierra's temperature down, though it didn't take the fever away completely until her episode was over. Make sure to find a flavor of the over the counter medicine that your child will take without putting up a fight. Chewable or dissolving strips might be an option for your child as well. You may want to consider suppositories for the episodes that include vomiting.

b) Having an acid reducer on hand will help alleviate some of your child's stomach issues and in some cases, Mylanta has been known to help with the mouth and throat sores.

c) Numbing agents, such as Orajel, for the mouth sores will help relieve your child's pain and can be purchased in different flavors.

d) Kids Be Kool gel sheets may make your fevering child more comfortable. These can be purchased online or at Walgreens. It's a simple strip that can be put on your child's forehead and used for up to 6 hours to provide a cool, soothing relief for hot foreheads.

4) Prescriptions – If you opted for Prednisone or another prescription drug, make sure that you have this on hand so that you are prepared for the next outbreak. Trying to coordinate filling prescriptions, while dealing with a sick child, can be overwhelming. You can also try mixing your prescription with Pediasure or another liquid to help make it easier for your child to take. Just be sure that the amount of liquid is small enough that your child will drink the entire amount. For pill forms of other prescriptions, mashing and mixing them in jelly, apple juice or honey* might be an option. Always ask your pharmacist for a flavoring option for your prescription liquids. You typically have to request it and it may cost a few dollars more, but it's worth it.

* Honey is not recommended for children under the age of two because it may contain a bacteria called Clostridium botulinum which causes infant botulism.

5) Favorite bear or stuffed animal – your child may already have a favorite bear or stuffed animal that you can easily grab, but another idea is to have a 'fever bear'. This is a stuffed animal that your child gets only when they are having their episode. It's a special stuffed animal that makes them feel special when they have it. Build-A-

Bear™ has some great options for bear clothing so that you can dress the bear in PJ's or a doctor's outfit.

6) <u>Electrolyte drinks</u> – when Sierra was fevering, it was sometimes hard to convince her that she needed to keep liquids in her system. Having pediatric electrolyte liquids on hand in flavors that your child enjoys will help keep them hydrated.

6. Preparing your child for a Tonsillectomy or T&A surgery

Sierra was very young at the time of surgery, so there wasn't too much conversation with her prior to surgery day. She did know she was going to the hospital so that the doctor could help her not be sick so often. I was careful not to promise her full health, not knowing what the results of the surgery would bring. As a parent, you know what information your child can handle, depending upon his or her age, but the best approach is to be honest and explain the need for the surgery and why you feel that this is important. One thing that did help explain to Sierra what a hospital stay was all about was a book she received from her grandmother called, *Franklin Goes to the Hospital.* Sierra wanted to read this book several times and each time she asked questions about her upcoming hospital visit which I answered. I think the open communication made her feel less anxious about her hospital visit.

Children's books

There are some great resources, all of which can be ordered on amazon.com or perhaps at your local library, for parents wanting to discuss surgery or a hospital visit with their child.

If you're looking for a general book on fevers, *Peeper Has A Fever* is an excellent choice. This book is for children between the ages of 2-7 experiencing a fever. The book was written by Dr. Charlotte Cowan, 2004. As a bonus, this book also includes a question and answer pamphlet on fevers for parents tucked in the back. I would highly recommend this book for young children.

For books on hospital stays, fevers or surgeries, I would recommend a choice from the following list:

- Cork, Barbara Taylor. 2002. *Katie Goes to the Hospital.*
- Cowan, Charlotte. 2005. *Peeper Has a Fever.*
- Hautzig, Deborah. 1985. *A Visit to the Sesame Street Hospital.*
- Jennings, Sharon. 2000. *Franklin Goes to the Hospital.*
- Johnston, Marianne. 1998. *Let's Talk About Going To The Hospital.*
- Karim, Roberta. 2002. *This is a Hospital, Not a Zoo!*
- Marsoli, Lisa Ann. 1985. *Things to Know Before You Go To The Hospital.*
- Monnig, Judy. 1987. *Coping With A Hospital Stay.* (for teens and adults)
- Rey, Margaret and H.A. 1966. *Curious George Goes to the Hospital.*
- Rogers, Fred. 1997. *Going to the Hospital.*
- Winthrop, Elizabeth. 1984. *Being Brave is Best (Tale from the Care Bears).*

❖   ❖

Other preparations

Involve your child in the grocery shopping ahead of time to make sure that after their surgery they have yummy and healthy treats to eat and their preferred liquids to ensure they stay hydrated.

Prepare a special bed for your child to have ready post surgery, either in their room or in the family room so that they can lay down and relax and watch TV when they get home from the hospital. Have books or coloring activities on hand so they can sit quietly. Your one-on-one attention and their need to feel special will help them to adjust to the requirement to keep their activity level down during their recuperation period.

Another thing to keep in mind is your child's fever cycle. Most ENT's will not perform a surgery if your child is fevering. If you are able to predict when the episode should occur, then schedule the surgery during a different date, away from your child's normal cycle.

Day of surgery

If your child knows that you are in support of the procedure and more importantly, doesn't see any visible anxiety or fear, he or she will most likely go into surgery knowing this is something that will make them feel better. Assure your child that you will be close by and that the procedure is very safe and that you trust your child's doctor.

For Sierra, I made sure to buy her 'special' pajamas. She was excited that day to wear her new pajamas to the hospital. It's likely that your hospital won't allow your child to wear their pajamas into surgery, but soon after the surgery, your child can change back into their special PJ's. I'd recommend bringing something that assures the child and makes him or her feel safe and comforted.

TIP: Most hospitals will allow your child to bring a special stuffed animal, doll or toy to comfort your child.

As your doctor may recommend, don't give your child any aspirin products within 10 days prior to the surgery and no ibuprofen or Advil within 7 days prior to surgery. Acetaminophen or Tylenol is usually acceptable, but always check with your doctor.

In most pediatric units, the nurses are so friendly and comforting to your child that their friendliness will help distract your child as you wait in the pre-operative room. There may be TV's in the room as well as books or other toys, which can easily work to entertain your child. Sierra's hospital bed actually had a steering wheel on the bed so she could pretend she was driving. Playing ahead of time helped keep Sierra's mind off of the purpose of our visit.

Sierra went directly from her pre-op hospital room to a hospital surgery waiting room with each unit separated by curtains. Sierra's Dad and I waited in this room for about 15 minutes until the nurse came to take Sierra into surgery.

During the procedure, your child may be given a mixture of gas and an intravenous medication for the general anesthetic. Sierra claims to still remember 'the mask' as she calls it, which breathed the sleepy air into her mouth. There will be no external incisions with this surgery and the surgery itself should take less than 60 minutes.

Upon completion, your child will be taken to the recovery room and may be discharged the same day, depending upon their age or medical situation. With Sierra, the whole procedure took just about half a day.

Once out of recovery, Sierra was wheeled back into the hospital room in which she started the day. She woke up screaming from her surgery in the recovery room and her nurse assured us that can be a common reaction for children waking up from anesthesia. Sierra was administered some Tylenol and soon fell back to sleep, waking up about 30 minutes later and feeling much better and more calm. It was strange seeing her go from full blown tears to her happy self after surgery. She was smiling and talking, though she did seem pretty tired. She slept much of the way home and was quiet for most of the day.

Recovery at home

Although Sierra's doctor didn't specifically recommend this, I would encourage elevating your child's pillow, which seems to help with any potential drainage. Additionally, and I cannot stress this enough, keep your child's medication regimen on schedule. Once the pain medication starts wearing off, it may be too late to get medicine into your child before extreme pain starts. Even though the most painful part of the surgery seems to be between days 4 and 10, the pain tends to creep up on small children who aren't always able to communicate their symptoms as they commence. Keep your child drinking fluids in whatever form that may be. It is recommended they drink about a ½ cup of fluids per hour at a minimum, if you're able to get them to agree with drinking this much. Make the process fun by having a special cup or using a shot glass or children's tea cup.

Call your child's doctor if you notice any bleeding, prolonged pain that isn't relieved by their prescribed medication, a fever greater than 101.5 degrees that persists after taking their medication, any sign of infection, dehydration, increased swelling or redness of neck, nose or eyes. It's better to call your doctor over a question that you might feel is insignificant than to risk not contacting your doctor and having the situation turn into a worse scenario.

❖   ❖

Foods to eat

It is not uncommon for your child to lose a little bit of weight during their recovery period, especially during days 4-10, when the pain is at its peak.

The following food and liquid suggestions may be helpful to have on hand prior to your child's surgery:

- Gelatin
- Ice cream
- Custard
- Pudding

- Mashed potatoes
- Snow cones
- Fruit smoothie
- PediaSure

You may be able to mix a small amount of protein powder in the ice cream, custard, fruit smoothie or pudding. Vanilla flavored protein powder is recommended as it seems to be pretty inconspicuous when mixed in with different foods. Keep in mind that milk products may produce phlegm and might not be the best choice for your child. Check with your child's doctor on food recommendations. Most hospitals will provide a post-op list of recommended foods for your child.

> **TIP:** I bought a snow cone maker and let Sierra pick out snow cone flavors prior to her surgery. This was a good way for her to keep liquids down and the shaved ice helped numb her throat as it was going down.

Remember, although you want your child to eat healthy, just keeping them hydrated and eating something should be the most important focus during their recovery.

❖   ❖

Days 4 – 10

This will not be a pleasant time period for your child's recovery. I can't tell you how many Yahoo PFAPA group posts I've seen about the difficulty in managing pain for the recovering child. Hang in there and know that you and your child will get through this time period. You may notice white patches on the back of their mouth which is representative of healing. As the scabs begin to fall off, there may be some bleeding. If you notice any bleeding longer than a few minutes, call your doctor. There will also be a noticeable smell or bad breath as your child's scabs disappear. Your child may notice a funny taste or bad smell. Just assure your child that this is normal. Keep the pain medication on schedule and try to administer the medication in advance of the pain getting to unbearable levels.

❖   ❖

Less common symptoms

Some children have been known to have post-operative night terrors, which seem to occur four days to two weeks after their surgery. If this is the case, comfort your child, keep an eye on the situation and let your doctor know if this symptom becomes a recurrent problem.

If bleeding, swelling or vomiting occurs, consult with your doctor.

7. Support Groups / Parenting Communities / Other Resources

PFAPA Yahoo support group –http://groups.yahoo.com/group/PFAPA
PFAPA online support and chat group. This is moderated and organized by Fran Bulone.

PFAPA Yahoo support group – Alternative treatments
http://groups.yahoo.com/group/PFAPA_Alternatives
This group is for families interested in exploring alternative medicine approaches to treating PFAPA diagnosed children. This group is intended to complement the mainstream medically-oriented PFAPA group. Topics discussed include homeopathic, naturopathic, chiropractic and any other unconventional approaches.

PFAPA.net
This site has been created to increase the knowledge on the PFAPA syndrome. It gives information on PFAPA syndrome for physicians, allied health professionals, patients and their family. This site is also aimed to help for research projects on PFAPA syndrome.

FMF Community – http://www.fmfcommunity.org
An informative site about many periodic fever diseases, including Familial Mediterranean Fever, FCAS, Muckle-Wells, NOMID, and many others.

Hyper-IgD & Periodic Fever Syndrome (HIDS) – http://hids.net
A good site dealing with HIDS, and has a link to the HIDS patient's platform.

CAPS Community – http://www.capscommunity.com
An informative site about Cryopyrin-Associated Periodic Fever Syndromes (CAPS) which includes NOMID, MWS and FCAS.

❖   ❖

Helpful sites for medical travel and lodging

PatientTravel.org – http://www.patientravel.org
PatientTravel.org is dedicated to helping assist patients in obtaining charitable long-distance medical air transportation or compassionate travel. They will help families needing to travel long distances fly to the medical facility that will care for the patient's needs. Take a look if you are seeking help for air travel to a medical center for your health condition.

Children's Inn at NIH (National Institutes of Health) –
http://www.childrensinn.org
A place for pediatric patients and their families to stay.

❖   ❖

Social Media Outlets

Twitter - @PFAPAChild
Follow @PFAPAChild to connect with other PFAPA parents. Make sure to mention through direct message or a tweet that you're a PFAPA family to get listed on the PFAPA family Twitter list.

Web – www.pfapachild.com. You can visit this site to order additional copies of this publication.

Shelby and Sierra

8. Medical Research and Articles

Chandy C. John, MD, MS and Janet R. Gilsdorf, MD, "**Recurrent fever in children**", Pediatr Infect Dis J, 2002;21:1071-80, Vol. 21, No. 11, copyright by Lippincott Williams & Wilkins, Inc., 2002.

Daniel L. Kastner, "**Hereditary Periodic Fever Syndromes**", Reprinted 2008, at http://asheducationbook.hematologylibrary.org/cgi/content/full/2005/1/74, American Society of Hematology, 2005.

Donald Schiff and Leslie L. Barton, **Tonsillectomy as a Therapeutic Option for PFAPA**", Reprinted 2008, at http://aapgrandrounds.aappublications.org, AAP Grand Rounds 2007; 18;66-67 DOI:10.1542/gr.18-6-66-a.

Greg Licameli, MD, MHCM; Jessica Jeffrey, MA; Jennifer Luz, BS; Dwight Jones, MD; Margaret Kenna, MD, MPH, "**Effect of Adenotonsillectomy in PFAPA Syndrome**", Reprinted at www.archoto.com, Arch Otolaryngology Head Neck Surg/Vol 134 (No. 2), February 2008.

Kenneth Tyson Thomas, BA; Henry M. Feder, Jr., MD; Alexander R. Lawton, MD; and Kathryn M. Edwards, MD, "**Periodic fever syndrome in children**", The Journal of Pediatrics, Vol. 135, No. 1, 1998.

Kevin K. Wong, MD; Jane C. Finlay, MD, FRCPC; J. Paul Moxham, MD, FRCSC, **"Role of Tonsillectomy in PFAPA Syndrome"**, Reprinted 2008, at http://archotol.ama-assn.org/cgi/reprint/134/1/16.pdf.

Shai Padeh, MD; Nava Stoffman, MD and Yackov Berkun, MD, **"Periodic Fever Accompanied by Aphthous Stomatitis, Pharyngitis and Cervical Adenitis Syndrome (PFAPA Syndrome) in Adults"**, IMAJ, Vol 10, May 2008.

9. Appendix

Fever Log Template / Information Sheet

Childs Name:_____
Date of Birth:_____
Primary Care Physician: _____
Specialty Care Physician(s):_____
Type of Specialty: _____
Date of initial PFAPA diagnosis (or periodic fever onset):_____

Cycle Notes	(Sample)	(Date)	(Date)
First date of onset	1/1/09		
Last date of onset	1/4/09		
Length of cycle	4 days		
Days from last cycle (1)	21		
Temperature range	101.1 – 103.2		
Symptoms	Lethargic, joint pain		
General Observations	Lack of appetite, full of energy when fever subsided, looked pale during episode		
Doctor Visits			
Primary / Specialty Doc visit	Yes - Primary		
Tests administered	Strep Test		
Results of tests	Negative		
Action taken	None – determined fever is PFAPA related		
General Comments			
General comments	Missed two days of school		

(1) Days from last cycle should calculate the days from last cycle "First" onset to the "First" onset of the next cycle

Sample Letter to Daycare Provider or School Teacher
This is a sample letter.

[Date]

Dear
School Name
1234 ABC Street
Anywhere, St 12345

Dear [Name]

As we discussed, [your child] has missed several days of school over the past several months due to her recurring fevers. [your child] was diagnosed *Periodic Fever, Apthous Stomatitis, Pharyngitis and Cervical Adenitis,* commonly referred to as PFAPA or Periodic Fever Syndrome. The good news is that [his/her] diagnosis is not a contagious illness as [his/her] doctor suggests in the attached note. The result of [his/her] fevers is due to an overactive immune system. The bad news is that the fevers are recurrent and have been appearing approximately every [No #] days.

[Your child] fevers may last anywhere from [No #] days and vary in intensity from a fever of [enter temperature]. [Your child's] symptoms may include [include symptoms]; therefore, there may be times that [he/she] is able to attend school and other times [he/she] will need to stay home and get some rest. Our family really appreciates you working with us to ensure that [your child] minimizes the time [he/she] is away from school.

I've attached an article on PFAPA so that you can read and learn about her diagnosis and educate [your child's] class, if necessary. It would also be helpful if you could pass my letter and information on to other staff members that would benefit by knowing about [your child's] condition. If you have any questions at all, please do contact me. Again, we very much appreciate your understanding and willingness to make [your child] feel comfortable in class.

Best regards,

Please note that bracketed sections should be completed with your child's specific information. It is suggested that you include with your letter a note from your child's doctor indicating the diagnosis and non-contagious nature of PFAPA as well as some brief information on PFAPA.

You may download a free copy of this letter from our website at **www.pfapachild.com**.

Glossary

Adenitis - inflammation of a gland or lymph node, which has the tendency to become enlarged or tender.

Adenoidectomy – A surgical procedure in which the adenoids are removed, often in conjunction with a tonsillectomy.

Aphthous Stomatitis - canker sores, or small ulcers, inside the mouth on the inner cheeks, lips or tongue.

Cimetidine – is a histamine H_2-receptor antagonist that inhibits the production of acid in the stomach. It is largely used in the treatment of heartburn and peptic ulcers. It is marketed by GlaxoSmithKline under the trade name Tagamet (sometimes Tagamet HB or Tagamet HB200) and was approved by the Food & Drug Administration for prescriptions starting January 1, 1979. (Definition from: Wikipedia).

Coblation Tonsillectomy – is a method used by ENT's to perform tonsillectomies, adenoidectomies and other surgical procedures.

This method uses radiofrequency, via a Coblation wand, to dissolve the affected tissue, while causing very little hard to surrounding tissue. This method was cleared by the U.S. Food and Drug Administration in 2001 and is trademarked by ArthroCare.

Colchicine - is a toxic natural product and secondary metabolite, originally extracted from plants of the genus *Colchicum* (Autumn crocus, *Colchicum autumnale*, also known as the "Meadow saffron"). Originally used to treat rheumatic complaints and especially gout, it was also prescribed for its cathartic and emetic effects. Its present medicinal use is mainly in the treatment of gout; as well, it is being investigated for its potential use as an anti-cancer drug. It can also be used as initial treatment for pericarditis and preventing recurrences of the condition. (Definition from: Wikipedia).

Febrile Seizure - According to the National Institute of Neurological Disorders and Stroke, febrile seizures are convulsions brought on by a fever in infants or small children. The child may loose consciousness and shake or it may be more on the mild side and show up as twitches in a portion of the body or on the left or right side only. These seizures may last as little as a few seconds or much as fifteen minutes or more.

FMV – Familial Mediterranean Fever.

HIDS – Hyperimmunoglobulinemia D Syndrome.

MEFV – Mediterranean Fever.

Periodic Fever - fevers occurring on a regular basis that last from two to six days and recur every three to eight weeks.

PFAPA – Periodic fever, aphthous stomatitis, pharyngitis and adenitis.

Pharyngitis - inflammation of the neck and throat to include the tonsils or larynx.

Prednisone - is a synthetic corticosteroid drug that is usually taken orally but can be delivered by intramuscular injection and can be used for a number of different conditions. It has a mainly glucocorticoid effect. Prednisone is a prodrug that is converted by the liver into prednisolone, which is the active drug and also a steroid. (Definition from: Wikipedia).

Singulair – is a prescription medicine approved to help control symptoms of asthma in adults and children 12 months and older and for relief of symptoms of indoor and outdoor allergies (outdoor allergies in adults and children as young as 2 years and indoor allergies in adults and children as young as 6 months). (Definition from: Singulair.com).

T&A – an acronym for the medical procedure of a Tonsillectomy and Adenoidectomy in which the tonsils and the adenoids are removed.

Tonsillectomy – A surgical procedure in which the tonsils are removed.

TRAPS – Tumor necrosis factor receptor-associated periodic syndrome.

Endnotes

[1]Department of Pediatric Otorhinolaryngology, Spedali Civili, Piazza Spedali Civili 1, 25123 Brescia, Italy, "Marshall's syndrome or PFAPA (periodic fever, aphthous stomatitis, pharyngitis, cervical adenitis) syndrome," January 2004, at http://www.orpha.net/data/patho/GB/uk-PFAPA.pdf.

[2]Donald Schiff and Leslie L. Barton, "Tonsillectomy as a Therapeutic Option for PFAPA," AAP Grand Rounds (2007), p.66; available at http://aapgrandrounds.aappublications.org.

[3]Greg Licameli, MD, MHCM; Jessica Jeffrey, MA; Jennifer Luz, BS; Dwight Jones, MD, Margaret Kenna, MD, MPH, "Effect of Adenotonsillectomy in PFAPA Syndrome", Arch Otolaryngol Head Neck Surg, Vol 134, (February 2008), available at www.archoto.com.

[4]Shai Padeh MD, Nava Stoffman MD and Yackov Berkun MD, "Periodic Fever Accompanied by Aphthous Stomatitis, Pharyngitis and Cervical Adenitis Syndrome (PFAPA Syndrome) in Adults," IMAJ (May 2008), p. 358.

[5]Kenneth Tyson Thomas, BA, Henry M. Feder, Jr., MD, Alexander R. Lawton, MD, and Kathryn M. Edwards, MD, "Periodic Fever Syndrome in Children," The Journal of Pediatrics (July 1999), p. 15-21.

[6]Dr. Daniel L. Kastner, American Society of Hematology, "Hereditary Periodic Fever Syndromes", 2005, at http://asheducationbook.hematologylibrary.org/cgi/content/abstract/2005/1/74.

Made in United States
Orlando, FL
13 May 2023

33120322R00055